OUR STOREHOUSE OF MISSOURI PLACE NAMES

ROBERT L. RAMSAY

UNIVERSITY OF MISSOURI PRESS   • COLUMBIA

TABLE OF CONTENTS

OUR STOREHOUSE OF
MISSOURI PLACE NAMES

COUNTIES OF MISSOURI

Beside the 114 counties on the present map, there were 15 earlier county names once adopted for a while, or proposed, or prevalent in popular usage:

ASHLEY COUNTY, 1843: changed officially in 1845 to **TEXAS COUNTY**

The **"BLUE COUNTRY",** before 1826, when it became **JACKSON COUNTY**

DECATUR COUNTY, 1843-1845: name adopted for two years by **OZARK COUNTY**

DODGE COUNTY, 1846: absorbed in 1853 by **PUTNAM COUNTY**

KINDERHOOK COUNTY, 1841: changed in 1843 to **CAMDEN COUNTY**

LAWRENCE COUNTY, 1815: dissolved in 1818 and divided into **WAYNE, MADISON,** and later into other counties, one of which, created in 1843, was the present **LAWRENCE COUNTY**

LILLARD COUNTY, 1820: changed in 1825 to **LAFAYETTE COUNTY**

NIANGUA COUNTY, 1841: changed in 1844 to **DALLAS COUNTY**

RIVES COUNTY, 1835: changed in 1841 to **HENRY COUNTY**

ROBERTS COUNTY, before 1839, when it became **BUCHANAN COUNTY**

ROLLINS COUNTY, 1856: name proposed for a new county that never materialized, to be formed out of parts of **BOONE, AUDRAIN, HOWARD, and RANDOLPH**

"SNAKE COUNTY", before 1849, when it became **McDONALD COUNTY**

The **"TWO RIVERS COUNTRY",** before 1826, when it became **MARION COUNTY**

VAN BUREN COUNTY, 1835: changed in 1848 to **CASS COUNTY**

WAKENDA COUNTY, 1833: name proposed but rejected in favor of **CARROLL COUNTY**

INTRODUCTION

Much can be learned about men and places from their names. A man's name reveals his family and his ancestry, often also his nationality and racial background, not infrequently his physical and spiritual inheritance and the hopes and ambitions that his parents had for him. Just so may the place names of a State disclose, under attentive and patient scrutiny, a host of hidden facts about its origins and traditions, the sources of its population, the circumstances of its settlement and subsequent history; about the men who made it and those who afterwards led it, about its geography, its flora and fauna and its soil, and about the ideals and culture of its people.

Names are fossil history. If the archaeologist can reconstruct, as he is so often able to do in older lands, and is now doing in Missouri with fascinating results, from a few dusty pots and tools and bones a whole series of dead and buried civilizations, so the student of language can find in the place names of the State equally priceless relics that are sometimes quite as old, and often even more revealing.

Place-name study is a young science, especially in America. Of course guessing about the origin of place names is old enough, just as is guessing about etymologies in general. Etymology never became a science till the days were over when Voltaire's famous definition of it had at last ceased to be so uncomfortably close to the truth. He defined etymology as speculation about the derivation of words, in which the consonants make very little difference and the vowels make no difference at all. That sort of etymology lasted considerably longer in the study of place names than it did for ordinary words. Even today, place-name derivations are not unknown of the sort satirized long ago by Shakespeare, when he made his Welsh captain Fluellen derive Monmouth from Macedon: because, in the first place, both names begin with an M; in the second place, "There is a river in Macedon, and there is also moreover a river at Monmouth"; and in the third place, "Alexander the Great was born in Macedon," and there are likewise "some goot men porn in Monmouth."

Just so, it is almost an article of faith with many Missourians that the name of their great river means the *"Big Muddy"*; that *Maries County* got its name from two mythical girls named Mary, and *Crève Coeur Lake* near St. Louis from a broken-hearted Indian maiden who drowned herself in its waters; that *Cape Cinque Hommes* on the Mississippi preserves the memory of five men who were once murdered there by the Indians; that the mysterious *One Hundred and Two River* in Nodaway County was so named because it is exactly 102 miles long, or else, as Mr. Homer Croy declares in one of his delightful novels, was given that name by the Mormons during their famous migration of 1847 because they crossed it just 102 miles from their last previous camp; or that the beloved name of the *Ozarks* signifies the land of bows or bends or curves, or even, as one informant confidently assured me, commemorates the real place where Noah's Ark landed after the Flood. There is not a shadow of truth in any one of these typical Missouri "tall tales," as will be shown in the following pages. Sentimentalists may regret the destruction of their fondest illusions; but they will find in these and many other cases that the truth is not only stranger than fiction, but often more interesting and even more romantic.

Basic Principles

The basic principles of modern place-name study, principles that at last entitle it to be called a science, are chiefly two. One of them is a respect for geography; the other is a respect for history. We have come to see that no reliable decision can safely be made about the origin of any place name until the place has actually been visited and its geographical situation and surrounding landscape observed. It is easy to sit in one's armchair and guess that the old town of *Eminence* in Shannon County must have got its name from being set on a hill; but when a visit reveals that the town is actually down in a hollow, considerable doubt is cast on the easy solution. Further research discloses that *Eminence* really borrowed its inappropriate name from another *Eminence,* now vanished, forty miles away that did stand on a conspicuous bluff. The actual length of the *One Hundred and Two River,* as the crow flies, from its source in Iowa to its mouth near St. Joseph, is only a little more than sixty miles. Even if one uses the little gadget that geographers call a "map-meter" to follow all its curves and meanders, it is impossible to make it more than 80 to 85 miles at the most. So many examples of this sort of error have been encountered in our studies, that we have adopted as an iron-clad rule that every place included in our survey with any such topographical or descriptive name must be visited and looked at before any opinion about its origin is expressed.

Even more important is the insistence on a respect for history, which means above all a respect for dates. We must find out, if we can, exactly when each place was founded and when it was named, and then consider what light is thrown upon the selection or invention of the name by contemporary or earlier events. Whenever the name has changed in form or substance, we must collect all the variants and arrange them in chronological order; for no place name can be adequately interpreted in the light of its present-day form alone, but must always be traced back so far as is possible to its earliest recorded or conjectural form. This is a counsel of perfection, which cannot always be carried out, for records are often missing or faulty.

It is especially human to err in the matter of dates; but with apologies for inevitable errors, our own included, the earliest date that could be found has been added in the present survey for almost every name included.

Many a mystery has been cleared up by consulting the earliest records. We know now, for example, that the *Maries River*, from which *Maries County* took its name, was at first spelled "Marais," a French word for "marsh" or "swamp," and had nothing to do with girls named Mary or Marie. *Cape Cinque Hommes* was originally written Cape St. Cosme, which happens to be pronounced in French in exactly the same way. It was obviously named for Father St. Cosme, who tells us himself in a letter dated 1699 how he had visited the spot in 1698 and erected a cross near by. A lucky find in the Kane manuscripts of 1847, now preserved at Stanford University, proves that the puzzling *One Hundred and Two River* was merely an American rendering of the older French name *Cent Deux,* applied to an Indian village near its headwaters. That French name, as I have surmised by a perhaps too bold conjecture, was an adaptation by the early French traders of the Indian name Çondse, meaning "hillside forest." The same Osage name, which we know was often used by them for one of their ancestral settlements, may have been manhandled in Callaway County by another French "popular etymology" into the equally puzzling name *Côte Sans Dessein.* The change was of course a rather violent one in both cases, but not more violent than their manipulation of "St. Cosme" into "Cinq Hommes," or the way the Americans in Cole County turned *Bois Brulé Creek* into the "Bob Ruley," or the Chenal Hubert in Lafayette County into the *Sniabar.*

Even stranger is the true story behind the name of *Crève Coeur Lake.* A study of early St. Louis history reveals that nearly a hundred years before the Missouri Crève Coeur is first recorded, there was a well known Crève Coeur Fort across the river in Illinois, founded by La Salle in 1689. The two Crève Coeurs must be connected, and doubtless the later one was transferred, like other French names and so many of the French people, after Illinois had to be surrendered by them to the British. Now La Salle's fort received its name just eight years after a notable military event in the home country. In 1672, during the War of 1670-78 between France and Holland, Louis XIV captured a famous Dutch fortress named Crèvecoeur. It is very probable that Le Salle named his New World fortress in Illinois in compliment to the victory of his royal master. The Netherlands fortress, in turn, is said to have been given its name by its defenders in a spirit of over-confident boasting: they called it Crèvecoeur because they were sure it was impregnable, i.e., a "heart-breaker" for attackers— a sort of Maginot Line, in fact. When it fell after just a few days' siege, of course their boast was remembered against them. So elated was King Louis over his unexpected triumph that he conferred a title of nobility on the successful French general, naming him Baron de Crèvecoeur. That surname was handed down to his descendants, one of whom, Hector Crèvecoeur by name, emigrated to America in 1754 and became a well known American author. So the name traveled from Holland to France, from France to Illinois, and then from Illinois to Missouri, carrying history with it that is really a good deal more romantic than the story about the heartbroken Indian maiden.

In the same way, the true origin of the name *Ozarks*, about which so much vain disputation has been indulged, has been settled once for all by an inspection of old French documents preserved in St. Louis. These speak often of hunting expeditions made by French fur-traders "aux Arcs," or "aux Os," or "aux Kans," i.e., into the territory of the Arkansas or Osage or Kansas tribes of Indians. It was the custom of the early French settlers to abbreviate the long Indian tribal names by using merely their first syllables.

It was another Indian tribe, the Missouris, who happened to be living near the mouth of the stream when Marquette came down the Mississippi in 1673, and who bequeathed their name to the river and the State. That name was the one applied to them by their bitterest enemies, the Fox tribe of Algonquins, who soon afterwards almost annihilated them. The name, in the Fox language, probably means "People with Big Canoes." The Missouris called themselves the Niutachi, which means "People Who Dwell at the Mouth of the River." Their name for the river itself, by the way, was Nishodse, which in the language used by all the Sioux tribes does mean "Muddy Water." So the familiar epithet of "Big Muddy" is not so far wrong after all. It is not the rightful meaning of *Missouri*, but that name was really conferred upon it by a series of pure accidents. But it is a fairly close rendering of the name by which it was known to the Indians who first lived upon its banks, the Missouris and the Osage.

What Has Been Done Elsewhere

Anything like scientific place-name study has barely begun in our country. We have been left far behind in this branch of research by our European colleagues. What may justly be called the modern investigation of place names began in 1864 with Isaac Taylor's readable, though not always reliable, volume entitled *Words and Places*. It has been carried further in Scandinavia than anywhere else in the world, as was revealed in 1928 by Olsen's magnificent study *Farms and Fanes of Ancient Norway: the Place Names of a Country Discussed in Their Bearings on Social and Religious History*. Much fruitful work has been done also in Germany, Italy, and France. A truly epoch-making contribution to the study was begun in 1924 by the English Place-Name Society with a volume entitled *An Introduction to the Survey of English Place Names*, by Allen Mawer and F. M. Stenton. They and their colleagues have continued in successive volumes, each one devoted to a single shire or county of England, and they have now covered considerably more than half of the country. Their methods are certainly the last word in modern scientific place-name study.

In contrast to these achievements abroad, we have done little more than set foot upon the fringe of our own field—the fruitful field afforded by the place names of the United States. Just how little has been accomplished is made manifest in the exhaustive and reliable index issued in 1948 by Richard B. Sealock and Pauline A. Seely under the title *Bibliography of Place-Name Literature in the United States, Canada, Alaska, and Newfoundland*. Most of the items included are scattered and fragmentary notes on individual names or those of particular regions. The compilers declare in their Preface: "There is no adequate dictionary of United States or Canadian place names. . . . Less than a dozen states have comprehensive scholarly guides to the origin and meaning of their names."

A brilliant and very readable popular introduction to our well-nigh untrodden territory was supplied in 1945 in the stimulating book by George R. Stewart entitled *Names on the Land.* Fairly comprehensive dictionaries have been produced for the place names of Arizona, California, Minnesota, Oregon, Pennsylvania, South Dakota, Washington, and West Virginia, the best and most scholarly probably being *South Dakota Place Names*, directed by Edward C. Ehrensperger in 1941, and *California Place Names: a Geographical Dictionary*, by Erwin G. Gudde in 1949. In Wisconsin, the names of a single county have found searching and exhaustive treatment by Frederick G. Cassidy in his *Place Names of Dane County*, published in 1941. Only last Christmas, at the 1951 meeting of the Modern Language Association in Detroit, an enthusiastic group of scholars from these and other states decided to organize for the first time a new and independent association, to be entitled the American Name Society, with the purpose of encouraging a more vigorous prosecution of investigation into the origin and history of every sort of American name and providing adequate means of publication.

Progress in the Study of Missouri Place Names

Our survey of Missouri place names began in 1928. By 1945, a series of as yet unpublished theses, numbering eighteen in all, had been produced by students in our Graduate School. In these the entire State has finally been covered. A complete list of these studies, with the counties included in each, is as follows:

1. 1928. Pace, Nadine. Central Counties: Boone, Callaway, Cole, Cooper, Howard, Moniteau, Saline.
2. 1928. Adams, Orvyl Guy. North Central Counties: Carroll, Chariton, Livingston, Linn, Macon, Grundy, Sullivan, Adair, Mercer, Putnam, Schuyler.
3. 1929. Ewing, Martha Kennedy. Northwest Counties: Buchanan, Clin-

ton, Caldwell, Daviess, De Kalb, Andrew, Holt, Atchison, Nodaway, Worth, Gentry, Harrison.

4. 1930. Myers, Robert L. Southwest Counties: Barton, Jasper, Newton, Cedar, Dade, Lawrence, Polk, Greene.
5. 1933. Bell, Margaret E. Southwest Border Counties: Webster, Wright, Christian, Douglas, Ozark, Taney, Stone, Barry, McDonald.
6. 1933. Johnson, Bernice Eugenia. West Central Counties: Bates, Cass, Henry, Johnson, St. Clair, Vernon.
7. 1933. Leech, Esther Gladys. East Central Counties: Randolph, Monroe, Audrain, Montgomery, Ralls, Pike.
8. 1937. Atchison, Anne. Five West Central Counties: Jackson, Lafayette, Platte, Clay, Ray.
9. 1938. Hamlett, Mayme Lucille. Six Southeast Counties: Pemiscot, Scott, Dunklin, New Madrid, Mississippi, Stoddard.
10. 1938. Elliott, Katherine. Six Northeast Counties: Marion, Shelby, Lewis, Knox, Clark, Scotland.
11. 1938. Weber, Frank T. Six South Central Counties: Miller, Pulaski, Osage, Maries, Phelps, Gasconade.
12. 1939. O'Brien, Anna. Five Central Southern Counties: Dallas, Laclede, Texas, Dent, Shannon.
13. 1939. Welty, Ruth. St. Louis and Jefferson Counties.
14. 1943. Overlay, Fauna Robertson. Five South Central Counties: Benton, Camden, Hickory, Morgan, Pettis.
15. 1943. Harrison, Eugenia L. Four River Counties: Franklin, Lincoln, St. Charles, Warren.
16. 1944. Zimmer, Gertrude M. Five Southeast Counties: Ste. Genevieve, St. Francois, Washington, Iron, Crawford.
17. 1945. Pottenger, Cora Ann. Five Southern Border Counties: Butler, Ripley, Carter, Oregon, Howell.
18. 1945. Hamlett, Mayme Lucille. Six More Southeast Counties: Perry, Cape Girardeau, Bollinger, Madison, Wayne, Reynolds.

These theses, though still only in typewritten form, are on the reserved shelves of the University of Missouri Library, where they are available to all who care to consult them. In addition, a grant was made in 1945 by the University Research Council for the preparation of a complete card file of all the names studied, totaling 32,324 for the entire State, with all the information, arranged in alphabetical order, that had been collected for each name by our hard-working students. This task was completed during the next two years, and the file placed in the University Library. Another copy of it, upon request, was sent in 1947 to the Board on Geographical Names of the Department of the Interior in Washington, D. C. It has been placed in the library there, where it is available to students from all parts of the country who may desire to consult it.

When the first seven theses were completed, in 1934, an *Introduction to a Survey of Missouri Place Names* was published in the University of Missouri Studies (IX, 1); and in 1941, upon the completion of the thirteenth thesis, a further report was made before the Missouri Academy of Science, entitled "Progress in the Survey of Missouri Place Names," and published in its *Proceedings* (vol. 7, no. 3).

Much remains to be done before our formidable task can be satisfactorily finished, in the way of sifting and condensing, checking and editing. There are hundreds of tantalizing problems still unsolved, and gaps and omissions of all sorts yet to be filled. Some progress in settling unanswered questions, so far as they are capable of being settled, has been made by the present writer in a series of "Place-Name Paragraphs"[1] which were written in popular form and published under the title "What's in a Name in Missouri," which appeared in Sunday editions of the *St Louis Globe-Democrat* from May 26, 1946, to Sept. 21, 1947. A number of articles on individual counties have also appeared in local newspapers, as follows:

"Place Names in Lawrence County," *The Lawrence Chieftain,* Mount Vernon, July 24, 1947

"Place Names of Taney County," *The Taney County Republican,* Forsyth, Sept. 7, 1950

"Some Secrets of Pemiscot Place Names," *The Democrat-Argus,* Caruthersville, Feb. 9 to March 16, 1951

"Some Secrets of Jefferson County Place Names," *The Jefferson Republic,* De Soto, March 29 to July 12, 1951

"Secrets of Franklin County Place Names," *The Washington Missourian,* July 5 to November 1, 1951

"Some Secrets of Boone County Place Names," *The Columbia Missourian,* November 6, 1951, to January 8, 1952

Our latest study to be published is entitled *The Pronunciation Guide to Missouri Place Names,* by Donald George Picinich, revised by R. L. Ramsay, in the University of Missouri Bulletin, Journalism Series no. 126 (vol. 52, no. 35), which appeared Dec. 10, 1951. This presented the actual pronunciation used by the leaders in each community for over eight hundred Missouri place names, recorded both in the International Phonetic Alphabet and by a special system of "Simplified Respelling." It will obviate the need in most cases of indicating the current pronunciations of the names listed in the present survey.

Scope of the Present Study

The present bulletin represents a further step in our slow progress toward the making of a complete and adequate dictionary of Missouri place names. This time an attempt will be made to cover the entire State, but only by the selection of important, typical, and representative names. A total of nearly 2000 names have been chosen. These include all the 114 counties, together with the earlier names once used by 15 of them; all of their county seats, and all towns which had a population of more than one thousand at

---

1 Some of the material in these paragraphs and articles has been used again in the present study.

the last census; all the larger and many of the older and more interesting rivers, lakes, and mountains; and about as many of the smaller places, whenever they help to fill out and illustrate the main classes of our names, or offer problems of particular suggestiveness. The little places, and names that have disappeared from present use, are often the ones most interesting and informative to students of the history of words. Names no longer employed are indicated by an asterisk in the Index.

Place names fall naturally into five main classes, though these classes often overlap and it is not always easy to draw a line between them. First are our borrowed names, taken from older places outside the State, both native and foreign. Local borrowings, from names of nearby places, are here excluded for lack of space, although Professor Cassidy has shown illuminatingly in his *Place Names of Dane County* how important and often how significant it is to know whether a name was first applied, as it was in the majority of cases, to a natural feature of the landscape such as a stream, lake, or mountain, and then transferred to man-made institutions or communities in its neighborhood, or whether it first arose from a church, school, farm, river landing, or early community, and spread therefrom to later and larger units. But it would require many more pages than we have at our command to discriminate the exact order of adoption of such local groups of names. Our present purpose will be served if these related names used in the same neighborhood are lumped together.

Second we have listed the historical and political names, coming from the Indians, the French and Spanish, or arising in the successive periods of American history. Personal names are here included so far as the persons honored by them helped to make our national or State history. These historical personages include our presidents, our national statesmen and leaders, our military and naval commanders and heroes, our Missouri governors and our State legislators and leaders.

Third come the local personal names, here restricted to persons known mainly in their own neighborhoods, local officials, professional men, citizens and landowners. Obviously it is not always easy to draw a line between local and larger prominence, but we have done the best we can. In any event it is always these local personages who have furnished by far the largest number of all our place names.

Fourth are what we have called the topographical names. These are the names given for location and description, flora and fauna, soil and mineral wealth, and also names of approbation or disapprobation.

Fifth and last come what may be denominated cultural names. These reflect the dominant ideals and aspirations and tastes of the namers. They include the literary, mythological, and religious names, and the very characteristic humorous names. With them have been placed names deliberately coined for various reasons.

A. BORROWED NAMES (343)

When occasion arises to choose a name for a newborn child, the most natural and usually the safest recourse is to name it "after" some older person, either a relative or some one else who is admired or loved. Just so in finding a name for a new place, the first thought of its founders is commonly to take over the name of the place from which they have come, or perhaps one from some distant land in which for one reason or another they are particularly interested. Hence the sources of our many Missouri borrowed names are an index both to the origins and to the affections of our Missouri people.

STOCK NAMES (22)

Columbia (county seat of Boone), 1819
Delmar (Henry), 1900
Delmar (Laclede)
Delmar Avenue (St. Louis)
Englewood (Boone)
Englewood (Jackson), 1892
Fairmont (Clark), 1864
Fairmount (Henry), 1857
Fairmount Park (Kansas City)
Farmington (county seat of St. Francois), 1825
Fredonia (Benton), 1896
Fredonia (Ray), 1869
Ingleside College (Marion), 1874
Inglesyde (St. Louis)
Lancaster (county seat of Schuyler), 1845
Lexington (Boone), 1818
Lexington (county seat of Lafayette), 1822
LINCOLN COUNTY, 1818
Manchester (St. Louis), 1825
Richmond (county seat of Ray), 1828
Sedalia (county seat of Pettis), 1857
Springfield (county seat of Greene), 1833

It is not always easy, or even possible, to identify the exact source from which a borrowed name has been taken. It may be an obvious loan, but one that came from any one of many different lenders. These so-called "stock" names, repeated in State after State, form a conspicuous feature of our American nomenclature. Such names have often been criticized as monotonous and indicative of a lack among us of originality and imagination. Why, it has been asked, do we need to have, in as many different states, 27 Washingtons, 26 Manchesters, and 23 Lincolns? As a matter of fact, there are actually 121 cities, towns, and villages named Washington in America, as tabulated by Professor Stewart in his *Names on the Land*, besides a State, 33 counties, 257 townships, and well nigh innumerable rivers, mountains, parks, schools, and streets. And yet there is another way of looking at these favorite American place names. Perhaps their constant re-currence in our country is due not so much to lack of originality as to our deep American sense of kinship and common inheritance.

These familiar and far-traveled names are indeed in a very real sense among the ties that bind us together as a distinctive nation. Some day, when we know more exactly the circumstances and dates of origin of the names in all our States, we can trace each step in the spread of these be-loved place names across the continent. We shall then be able to construct for every one of them a chart, perhaps with arrows running from each origi-nal name-father to his brood of place-name children, that will give us a series of vivid pictures of the growth of our country. Behind each one of these seemingly commonplace names lies a story of what has been happily called "progressive pioneering" in the development of America.

Let us take for example one of these "unoriginal" names found today in at least twenty-five different States—the name of *Lexington*. All our Ameri-can Lexingtons are the spiritual children of an obscure little Massachusetts village that slept unnoticed by its neighbors for the first hundred and fifty years after its founding. But in 1775, when the first shot in the Revolu-tionary War was fired in that same little village, it sprang suddenly into the hearts of all Americans, as the cradle and symbol of our liberty.

That very year, in Kentucky a thousand miles away, a party of hunters heard the electrifying news, and decided at once to adopt the name. That was our second Lexington. The older Southern States, never backward in their admiration for real Yankee grit, were close behind Kentucky. Lexing-ton in Virginia, the county seat of Rockbridge in the heart of the Valley, was settled and christened in 1778. From there the name spread rapidly to North and South Carolina, Georgia, Florida, Alabama, Mississippi, Tenne-see, Arkansas, and Texas, till it has now become every bit as much Southern as Northern. Meanwhile it was carried to Maine, New York, and Pennsyl-vania, and then across the Appalachians to Ohio, Indiana, Illinois, and Michigan.

Kentucky men carried it first to Missouri, where it was adopted in 1818 for the first settlement made in the present Boone County, in the center of the State. Boone County was settled almost entirely by incoming Ken-tuckians, who poured in to what is still known as the "Boone's Lick Coun-try" just after the conclusion of the War of 1812. It is strongly suspected that this first settlement, established there two years before Boone became a separate county, chose the revered name of Kentucky's first capital with hope of thereby clinching its ambition to become the county seat. If so, it was disappointed. The coveted prize went instead to another town in the center of the county which had craftily chosen for itself a name—perhaps the only conceivable name—that was even more patriotic than *Lexington*. That was the name of *Columbia*.

The defeated Boone County *Lexington* pined away soon afterwards and disappeared from the map. Promptly upon its demise, the precious name was eagerly appropriated, in 1822, for the seat of the younger county of La-fayette, a little farther to the west. Before long, Missouri men helped to take it on to Iowa, Nebraska, Oklahoma, and Kansas, till at last it reached the Pacific Coast in Oregon. Surely the thread that ties all our Lexingtons together is a potent strand in the warp and woof of the very fabric of America.

Even more pervasive has proved the name that ousted *Lexington* from Boone County. *Columbia,* unlike *Lexington,* sprang not from a place but from a poem. It was first used, and probably first coined, by Philip Freneau in 1775 in his youthful poem entitled "American Liberty." Freneau wrote it under the stirring impulse of the news that had just come from Lexington, while Boston was still under siege.

What madness, Heaven, has made Britannia frown?
Who plans or schemes to pull Columbia down?

wrote the impassioned young patriot; then, perhaps apprehensive lest his daring coinage might not be understood, he affixed an explanatory footnote:

Columbia, America sometimes so called
from Columbus, the first discoverer.

This leaves it a bit uncertain whether Freneau actually invented the name, or whether he merely plucked it, so to speak, out of the air of that electric period. Perhaps he could not have told which it was himself. But certain it is that Freneau's is the first recorded use of it.

Freneau's new name for the new country received at first an enthusiastic welcome from his fellow-countrymen. In 1778, that stout old Tory, Presi-dent Myles Cooper of King's College in New York City, was stripped and beaten by an indignant mob of patriots, and barely managed to escape with his life to a British ship-of-war in the harbor. Promptly the institution he left behind him changed its too royalist name to *Columbia University.* The name came nearest to adoption for the country as a whole in 1791, when the commissioners appointed to lay out the nation's capital decided to call its neutral federal territory the *District of Columbia.*

But Freneau's name incurred a fatal setback in 1819, when one of our good neighbors to the south took it away from us by deciding to call itself Colombia. *Columbia* and Colombia were altogether too much alike. Since then, as a national name, *Columbia* has been increasingly relegated to poetry and silver-tongued oratory. Perhaps it was always too poetical a name for our practical-minded people; or perhaps Freneau was not quite a great enough poet.

For smaller centers of population, however, the poetical *Columbia* has enjoyed an immense success, multiplying miraculously till it has been adopted by towns in thirty-two States, not to mention innumerable counties, townships, schools, parks, and a great western river. The first town to adopt the name was the new capital of South Carolina in 1786. Soon all the ten states south of the Mason and Dixon line had their Columbias, as have six states in the Northeast, ten in the Middle West, and six in the West. We do not yet know the exact order of time for all the other Columbias that followed the lead of South Carolina. We do know that the name reached Boone County, Missouri, in 1819, probably brought there direct from Columbia, Kentucky, the seat of Adair County. Its adoption by the canny founders of a village which originally had the prosaic name of *Smithton* helped it not only to win the coveted prize of county seat, but also the location of the State University.

When it became apparent that Freneau's coinage of a substitute for our cumbersome national name of "United States of America" had finally failed of adoption, many and desperate were the attempts to find another "ersatz" name to fill a need that has always been deeply felt. Among them were Washingtonia, Usona, Appalachia, Atlantis, and Fredonia. None of them really ever had a chance of success; but the one that appealed most widely, next to Columbia, was *Fredonia*.

That name was suggested shortly before 1800 by Dr. Samuel Latham Mitchell of New York. Its hybrid and barbarous derivation was against it from the start. Mitchell was never able to decide whether it meant a "free gift," or the land where things are "freely done." But is was formed on the familiar pattern of Caledonia, Laddonia, and others -donias, and it seemed to signify the "land of freedom." So it won a considerable degree of popularity. It spread to at least eighteen states, all the way from New York, where it started, to Arizona and Texas. Probably it reached Missouri by way of Kentucky or Tennessee. Our *Fredonia* came first to Ray County in 1869, where a town was laid out intended especially for Negro freedmen; but it never developed. Another *Fredonia* arose in Benton County in 1896; but it too declined and disappeared after a few years. Perhaps Missourians feel they have enough freedom already, and do not need to be reminded of it.

The interwoven strands of Northern and Southern inheritance in the fabric of Missouri are nowhere better exemplified than our two place names *Springfield* and *Richmond*. One of these fine names has carried clear across the continent the sharp ineradicable flavor of New England; the other has taken from Atlantic to Pacific the warm memories and associations of the Old South.

Our twenty-six American Springfields have all issued from the loins of an ancient village in Essex, England, so small that it no longer appears at all on most maps. A Puritan who once lived there, William Pyncheon, came over in 1636 to Massachusetts and helped to found a new settlement in the new land, which probably at his suggestion took the name of his home town. Long afterwards, when it began to grow into a great industrial city, a brood of little Springfields borrowed its name in all the neighbor States: New Hampshire, Vermont, and Maine, New York, New Jersey, and Pennsylvania.

Then it spread southward to Maryland, West Virginia, North Carolina, Georgia, and Louisiana, and across the mountains to Tennessee and Kentucky. At about the same time the second largest city of the name was founded in Ohio, and the third largest in Illinois, to become the capital of that State. The fourth largest *Springfield* in size of all the sisterhood arose in Missouri.

Our Missouri *Springfield* adopted the name in 1833. The most authentic account tells us just how it was done. "Everybody in Greene County was invited to come in and vote their choice of a name for the county seat. James Wilson had a jug of white whiskey; and as fast as the people came in, he took them over to his tent and said: 'I am going to live here. I was born and raised in a beautiful little town in Massachusetts named Springfield; and it would please me very much if you would go over and vote to name this town *Springfield.*' Then he produced the jug . . ." Needless to say, Wilson had his way.[1]

No doubt it was other Missouri men and homesick New Englanders, with their persuasive whiskey jugs, that carried the name on to Arkansas, Kansas, Nebraska, Wisconsin, Minnesota, South Dakota, Colorado, and at last all the way to Oregon.

Our twenty-seven *Richmonds,* when properly hooked together, form a contrasting but equally potent thread in the weaving of our nation. Their name came from Richmond on the Thames, ancient site of an English royal palace. There is a group of Northern Richmonds, probably starting from New York and spreading thence to Massachusetts, New Hampshire, Vermont, and Maine, also to Pennsylvania, Michigan, and Wisconsin. But it was the city founded in Virginia in 1733 by Colonel William Byrd, and so named by him from a fancied resemblance to the town near London where he had once resided, that became name-mother to most of our later American Richmonds.

Thence it was taken south to North Carolina, Georgia, Alabama, Mississippi, and later to Texas and Arkansas; then step by step to Ohio, Indiana, and Illinois. In 1828 it reached Missouri, to become the county seat of Ray County, named, we are told, directly from Richmond, Virginia.

1 Wilson's Creek, the site of the bloodiest battle of the Civil War fought in Missouri, was named for James Wilson.

From Missouri it spread west to Iowa, Kansas, Oklahoma, Minnesota, Utah, and Washington. And wherever Richmond has gone, it was felt to be and still remains the symbol and hallmark of Dixieland.

Another classic example of "progressive pioneering" is afforded in the authentic account of the naming of *Lincoln County* in 1818. The first permanent American settler in the county, and the man responsible for its name, was Major Christopher Clark. He was born in North Carolina in 1766, and came out to Missouri in the first years of the 19th century. He was a genuine frontiersman, and when he became a member of the Territorial Legislature in 1818, he made himself an earnest advocate of the establishment of the new county. He made a speech which is reported as follows: "Mr. Speaker, I'm in favor of the new county. I was born in Lincoln County, North Carolina; I have lived a year or so in Lincoln County, Kentucky; and I want to live and die in Lincoln County, Missouri." His speech was loudly applauded, and the county was organized and named as he desired.

Major Clark may have been unaware that there are Lincoln Counties also in at least 18 other States besides North Carolina, Kentucky, and Missouri. At the same time, it is likely that the members of the 1818 Legislature had in mind the Revolutionary War hero for whom all the Lincoln Counties that came into existence before 1860 were probably named, General Benjamin Lincoln, who had died only a few years before. General Lincoln (1733-1810) of Massachusetts had served with distinction throughout the Revolution. He was a special friend of Washington, who deputized him to receive the sword of Cornwallis on his surrender at Yorktown in 1781. He was Secretary of War for the Continental Congress from 1781 to 1783. Such a place name must receive a double classification. It was certainly borrowed from Kentucky and North Carolina. Just as certainly it belongs likewise under our category of historical names chosen in honor of our famous American military leaders.

Other stock names in Missouri whose provenance it is not easy to trace are *Manchester,* one of twenty-six, which came to St. Louis County in 1825; *Lancaster,* one of twenty, which became county seat of Schuyler in 1845; and *Farmington,* one of twenty-five, which was made county seat of St. Francois in 1825. The descriptive name of *Fairmount* has been adopted in eighteen States, Missouri's *Fairmount Park* in Jackson County being probably borrowed direct from Fairmount Park in Philadelphia. The name of *Delmar* in Laclede and Henry Counties was probably taken from that of *Delmar Avenue* in St. Louis, and is shared by ten other States. That of *Englewood* in Boone County we know to have been a loan from Englewood, Illniois; but it is found also in eight other States. Its prettier substitute of

Inglesyde, in Marion and St. Louis Counties, was adopted in six other States.

The rule has naturally been that these place-name favorites have started in the East and spread westward. One solitary exception, unique so far as I am aware, started here in Missouri and spread therefrom both eastward and westward. That was the name of *Sedalia.* We know definitely that it was deliberately coined by General George R. Smith in 1857. He named it for his youngest daughter Sarah, who was known familiarly to her family and friends by the pet-name of "Sed." His first thought was to call the town "Sedville;" but that name, he decided on second thought, would hardly "comport with the large and flourishing city of his dreams." He was right, for Sedville is decidedly lacking in appeal. Then the inspiration came to him to name the new county seat of Pettis *Sedalia.* That name seems to have had a compelling charm for many other Americans. From Missouri it has spread to fourteen other States: eastward to Kentucky and Tennessee, Indiana and Ohio, Virginia, North and South Carolina, and Florida; and southward and westward to Arkansas and Oklahoma, Colorado and North Dakota, Texas and Washington. Perhaps it has the right, on the strength of the record, to be acclaimed as Missouri's most beautiful place name.

This list of what may be called contagious place names found in Missouri might be extended almost indefinitely. It would certainly include most of the places named for our presidents, national statesmen and war heroes, and many others. But until all the States have achieved the much to be desired goal of producing adequate dictionaries of their names, we cannot possibly draw up a reliable list of such general loans, or of the channels by which they reached us. Under the circumstances, all we can do is to list all these borrowings once more according to what seems to have been their immediate source, if we have any trustworthy evidence to determine it. If not, we have adopted what may seem the doubtful policy of assigning the loan to Kentucky or Tennessee if the name is found in either or both of these parental commonwealths.

NAME-CHILDREN OF KENTUCKY (66)

The familiar claim that Kentucky is to be considered the mother of Missouri, though it has been vigorously contested because so many early Missourians came from other States, finds considerable support in our place names. It is to be understood in the same sense in which we speak of England as our mother country, even though many of our finest American families and greatest leaders have come from other countries. Just so, as we shall see below, many Missouri place names, including some of the oldest, were borrowed from other States; but Kentucky leads all the rest by a large margin. Of our 114 counties, thirty-six have names presumably, or at least possibly, taken from Kentucky. In Boone County alone, where more than 30 places adopted borrowed names, all but a single one came, more or less certainly, from Kentucky.

We must say "more or less certainly," because as stated above some of them may have been adopted independently in Missouri, like the name of Boone County directly from Daniel Boone himself, or like Lexington from another Lexington in one of the older States. Such names must receive a double classification. But every one of the sixty-six names listed here was used in Kentucky first before it was adopted in Missouri.

It is also true that a good many of our old Kentucky names have disappeared from our present-day map, for the Kentucky influence has undoubtedly diminished in the course of time. These vanished names have all been starred in the Index at the end of this Bulletin. Dates of founding or naming have been added wherever available.

ADAIR COUNTY, 1841
Ashland (Boone), 1853
BOONE COUNTY, 1820
Boonesborough (Boone), 1836
Boonsboro (Howard), 1840
Boonville (Cooper), 1817
Bourbon or Bourbonton (Boone), 1825
Bowling Green (county seat of Pike), 1820
Buena Vista (Boone), 1825
Burlington (Boone), 1856
BUTLER COUNTY, 1849
Butler (Boone),
CALDWELL COUNTY, 1836
CARROLL COUNTY, 1833
CARTER COUNTY, 1859
CHRISTIAN COUNTY, 1859
CLAY COUNTY, 1822
Claysville (Boone), 1844
CLINTON COUNTY, 1833
Columbia (Boone), 1819
DAVIESS COUNTY, 1836
Eureka (Boone),
FRANKLIN COUNTY, 1818
Fredonia (Ray), 1869
Fredonia (Benton), 1896
Ginlet (Boone) (for Gimlet, Ky.)
HARRISON COUNTY, 1845
HENRY COUNTY, 1841
JACKSON COUNTY, 1826
JEFFERSON COUNTY, 1818
JOHNSON COUNTY, 1834
KNOX COUNTY, 1845

LAWRENCE COUNTY, 1815
LAWRENCE COUNTY, 1843
Lebanon (Boone), 1836
Lexington (Boone), 1818
Lexington (Lafayette), 1822
LINCOLN COUNTY, 1818
LIVINGSTON COUNTY, 1837
Louisville (Lincoln), 1832
MADISON COUNTY, 1818
MARION COUNTY, 1826
Maysville (county seat of De Kalb), 1845
Melbourne (Boone)
MERCER COUNTY, 1845
MONROE COUNTY, 1831
MONTGOMERY COUNTY, 1818
MORGAN COUNTY, 1833
Oldham (Boone)
Paris (county seat of Monroe), 1831
PERRY COUNTY, 1820
Petersburg (Boone), 1836
PIKE COUNTY, 1818
Pineville (county seat of McDonald), 1847
Providence (Boone), 1844
PULASKI COUNTY, 1833
Rock Bridge (Boone),
SCOTT COUNTY, 1821
SHELBY COUNTY, 1835
Silver Fork (Boone), 1816
Sturgeon (Boone), 1856
Summerville (Boone), 1848
WARREN COUNTY, 1833
WASHINGTON COUNTY, 1813
WAYNE COUNTY, 1818
WEBSTER COUNTY, 1855

NAMES FROM TENNESSEE, VIRGINIA, AND NORTH CAROLINA (23)

Tennessee has some right to be called a second mother of Missouri, especially for its southern part; and Virginia may well claim to be its grandmother. Many of our Kentucky names listed above came originally from Virginia, as was the case with Lebanon, Petersburg, and Rock Bridge; but all of them probably came to us direct from the Blue Grass. Names almost certainly taken from these three other parental States are as follows:

Tennessee:
Bolivar (county seat of Polk), about 1840
Chilhowee (Johnson), 1858
DE KALB COUNTY, 1845
GREENE COUNTY, 1833
GRUNDY COUNTY, 1841
Knoxville (Ray), 1845

Lebanon (county seat of Laclede), 1853
MACON COUNTY, 1837
Memphis (Scotland), 1837
Nashville (Boone), 1819
Nashville (Barton), 1869
POLK COUNTY, 1835
PUTNAM COUNTY, 1845
SULLIVAN COUNTY, 1843

Virginia:

Richmond (county seat of Ray), 1828
Richmond Heights (St. Louis), 1896
Roanoke (Randolph), 1836
Luray (Clark), 1860
Virginia (Bates), 1871

North Carolina:

Buncombe (Franklin), 1842
Buncombe (Pettis), 1870
Buncomb Ridge (Butler and Ripley)
CAMDEN COUNTY, 1843

The Buncombe names come from Buncombe County, North Carolina, which in turn was named for a brave soldier of the Revolutionary War (see below, pages 57 and 58).

OTHER SOUTHERN NAMES (12)

Maryland:

Annapolis (Iron), 1876
Maryland Heights (St. Louis), 1926

South Carolina:

Beaufort (Franklin), 1849
Charleston (county seat of Mississippi), 1837

Georgia:

Gainesville (county seat of Ozark), 1841
DECATUR COUNTY (Ozark), 1843-1845
(from Decatur, Ga.)

Alabama:

Anniston (Mississippi), 1895
Tallapoosa (New Madrid), 1902
Tuscumbia (county seat of Miller), 1837

Mississippi:

Vicksburg (Pemiscot), 1915

Louisiana:

Iberia (Miller), 1842
Port Hudson (Franklin), 1859

NAMES FROM OUR NORTHERN NEIGHBORS (23)

Illinois:

Alton (county seat of Oregon), 1862
Cairo (Randolph), 1858
Englewood (Boone)

Kewanee (New Madrid), 1910
Peoria (Washington), 1910
Urbana (Dallas), 1867
Vandalia (Audrain), 1871
Westalton (St. Charles), 1896

Indiana:
Avilla (Jasper), 1858

Ohio:

Akron (Harrison), 1858
Bucyrus (Texas), 1899
Canton (Lewis), 1853
Celina (Dent), 1860
Chillicothe (county seat of Livingston), 1837
Greenville (county seat of Wayne), 1819
Lucerne (Putnam), 1887
Ravanna (Mercer), 1857
Xenia (Nodaway)), 1845

Iowa:
Oskaloosa (Barton)

Wisconsin:
Boscobel (Dent)
Koshkonong (Oregon), 1882

Michigan:
Saginaw (Newton), 1890

Canada:
Toronto (Camden), 1832

NAMES FROM EASTERN AND NEW ENGLAND STATES (30)

Pennsylvania:
Catawissa (Franklin), 1858
Sabula (Iron), 1886

New Jersey:
Newark (Knox), 1837
Passaic (Bates), 1891
Princeton (county seat of Mercer), 1846
Trenton (county seat of Grundy), 1841

New York:
Albany (county seat of Gentry), 1857
Buffalo (county seat of Dallas), 1841
Elmira (Ray), 1887
New York (Shelby), 1835
New York (Scott), 1844
Olean (Miller), 1881
Plattsburg (Clinton), 1835
Rennsalaer (Ralls), 1876
Syracuse (Morgan), 1867
Tuxedo (St. Louis), 1895
Troy (county seat of Lincoln), 1825
Utica (Livingston), 1837

Connecticut:
 New Hartford (Jefferson), 1805
 New Haven (Franklin), 1858

Massachusetts:
 Chicopee (Carter), 1888
 Granby (Newton),
 Lexington (Lafayette), 1822
 Malden (Dunklin), 1877
 New Boston (Linn), 1846
 Plymouth (Carroll), 1881
 Springfield (county seat of Greene), 1833
 Worcester (Audrain), 1886

New Hampshire:
 Nashua (Clay), 1891

Maine:
 Casco (Franklin), 1871

These names from the North and East arrived, as the dates indicate, on the whole distinctly later than did the Kentucky and other Southern names. The majority of the loans from below the Mason and Dixon Line were domiciled in Missouri in the early decades of the Nineteenth Century. Those coming from above the Line entered mainly in the middle decades, though there are some striking exceptions in such early Northern names as New Hartford and Troy, Greenville and Springfield.

NAMES FROM WESTERN STATES (30)

Kansas:
 Leavenworth (Platte)
 Olathe (Douglas), 1895

Nebraska:
 Omaha (Putnam), 1879

Montana
 Anaconda (Franklin), 1892

Alaska:
 Yukon (Texas), 1900

Washington:
 Spokane (Christian), 1893

Oregon:
 Oregon (county seat of Holt), 1841
 OREGON COUNTY, 1845

Texas:
 TEXAS COUNTY, 1845
 Cisco (Livingston),
 El Paso (Atchison), 1852
 Houston (county seat of Texas), 1857
 Laredo (Grundy), 1887

Palopinto (Benton), 1876
Passo (Benton), 1899 (for El Paso?)
San Antonio (Buchanan), 1850
Waco (Jasper), 1875

New Mexico:
Brazito (Cole), 1850
Santa Fé (Monroe), 1836
Santa Fé Trail (from Franklin in Howard
County to Santa Fe, New Mexico), 1804
Taos (Cole), 1849

California:
California (county seat of Moniteau), 1846
Chula Vista (Taney), 1930
Coloma (Carroll), 1858
La Jolla Park (Franklin),
Nevada (county seat of Vernon), 1855 (from
Nevada County, Calif., not from the State)
Topaz (Douglas), 1894
Wyreka (Putnam), 1858
Yuma (Putnam), 1893

The West as a whole:
Pacific (Franklin), 1854

This last mentioned town embodies in its name the essential spirit of the great westward movement, which was closely bound up with the coming of the railroads. When the new town was first laid out in 1852, it was named *Franklin,* for the county. It was planned as a station on the projected new railway, which had been christened, somewhat prematurely, the Atlantic & Pacific Railroad. The story goes that when the road was begun at St. Louis in 1851, the hope was that it would soon reach the Pacific Ocean. But progress was slow, and obstacles multiplied. It was 1853 before thirty-seven miles of track were laid and a train ran all the way across St. Louis County to the borders of Franklin. Once arrived at the new town, it stopped there for two more years. Meanwhile, when the station at the end of the line made application for a postoffice, it was discovered that there was already a town of *Franklin* in Howard County, founded back in 1816, and a new name had to be selected. Finally the name of *Pacific* was chosen, in honor of the hoped-for terminus of the future highway. The road dropped the Atlantic part of its name and became the Missouri Pacific Railroad, as it is still known today. It could already claim to run from (or in) Missouri to one Pacific, even though it was a good many years before it reached the other Pacific.

The Prophet Mahomet is said once to have commanded a mountain to come to him. When it failed to move as ordered, he sensibly decided that it would be sufficiently satisfactory if Mahomet moved to the mountain.

Our pertinacious ancestors had more faith than Mahomet—or perhaps a keener sense of humor. When they found that they could not move on to the Pacific Ocean quite as soon as they had hoped, they calmly moved Pacific some two thousand miles closer to St. Louis.

OTHER AMERICAN NAMES (14)

To these Western names may be added the many that have been borrowed from Spanish America:

Mexico:

>**Mexico** (county seat of Audrain), 1836
>**Buena Vista** (Platte), 1841
>**Molino** (Audrain), 1847
>**Monterey** (Reynolds), 1895
>**Vera Cruz** (Douglas), about 1850
>**Yucatan** (Callaway)

West Indies:

>**Cuba** (Crawford), 1867
>**Havana** (Gentry)
>**Hayti** (Pemiscot), 1894

South America:

>**Bolivia** (Ste. Genevieve), 1830
>**Brazil** (Washington), 1891
>**Callao** (Macon), 1858
>**La Plata** (Macon), 1855
>**Potosi** (county seat of Washington), 1814

The beautiful Spanish names scattered over our State from end to end came to us in three periods. The first and smallest group were introduced by the Spanish themselves from old Spain before the Louisiana Purchase, like *Nueva Madrid* in 1788 or *El Camino Real,* named in honor of King Charles IV of Spain in 1789; or else were adopted shortly afterwards by Americans who were still in close and friendly relations with the Spanish, like the names of the great *Santa Fé Trail* or the mining center of *Potosi,* borrowed from the famous silver mines in Bolivia.

The flood came with the Mexican War. The first place name of this second group to be adopted was that of the town of *Mexico,* just as the threat of that war was appearing on the horizon. The war itself brought in successive order *Buena Vista, Molino, Taos, Vera Cruz, Brazito, San Antonio,* and *El Paso,* and later at uncertain dates *Laredo, Cisco, Palopinto, Monterey,* and *Yucatan.* All of these were named for places in Mexico itself or its former possessions.

The climax arrived with the gold rush in California in 1849. Returning prospectors brought back dozens of Spanish names along with their precious gold dust. Among them are *Coloma,* for the California town where gold was first discovered, and *Yuma, Chula Vista, Wyreka* (with a special Missouri spelling for Yreka), *Nevada,* and *California* itself. Some of these Western names are of course Indian in origin; but all of them had become Spanish in dress.

FOREIGN PLACE NAMES (123)

We have listed over two hundred borrowed names of American origin. Over a hundred others were borrowed from across the seas. There are of course many foreign names by origin in the American lists given above; but those below were taken straight from abroad. First we shall list the names that come from what we still call the "Mother Country":

NAMES FROM THE BRITISH ISLES (26)

England:

Belvoir (Vernon), about 1840
Birmingham (Clay), 1887
Bristol (Jackson), 1889
Brosely (Butler), 1915
Brunswick (Chariton), 1836
Chelsea (S. Louis)
Dover (Lafayette), 1839
Exeter (Barry), 1880
Falmouth (Lincoln), 1836
New London (county seat of Ralls), 1819
Oxford (Worth)
Saint Albans (Franklin), 1837

Scotland:

Aberdeen (Pike), 1891
Argyle (Osage)
Athol (Jackson)
Caledonia (Washington), 1819
Edina (county seat of Knox), 1839
Edinburg (Scotland), about 1837
Kilwinning (Scotland), 1886
Montrose (Henry), 1871
SCOTLAND COUNTY, 1841

Wales:

New Cambria (Macon), 1864

Ireland:

Belfast (Newton), 1880
Dublin (Barton)
Sligo (Crawford), 1886
Tyrone (Texas), 1892

Most of these have become stock names, found also in many other States. Scotland has a surprisingly large part in Missouri nomenclature, brought in by the devoted and pertinacious Scotchmen who have played so notable a part in the life and history of our State. When Scotland County was organized, the old Scottish surveyor, S. W. B. Carnegy, persuaded the settlers to adopt the name of his homeland, besides christening two of the new settlements Edinburg and Kilwinning, and even calling two freshly formed townships Maidenkirk and Ayreshire. Other Missouri Scots have been equally mindful of "Auld Lang Syne."

NAMES FROM LATIN LANDS (44)

Together with the place names borrowed from Romance countries have been listed here, as the most convenient category, our places named for famous Frenchmen, Spaniards, and Italians and their homes.

France:
> Argonne (Lafayette), 1918
> Chantilly (Lincoln), 1876
> Elba (Dent), 1899
> Gasconade River, before 1800
> **GASCONADE COUNTY**, 1820
> La Grange (Lewis), 1836
> **LAFAYETTE COUNTY**, 1825
> Longwood (Pettis), 1852
> Metz (Vernon), 1870
> Moselle (Franklin), 1860
> Napoleon (Lafayette), 1836
> Normandy (St. Louis), 1876
> Paris (county seat of Monroe), 1831
> St. Helena (once county seat of Pettis), 1833
> Strasburg (Cass), 1875
> Versailles (county seat of Morgan), 1834
> Vichy (Maries), 1880
> Urich (Henry), 1871

Belgium:
> Belgique (Perry), 1890
> Brussels (Lincoln), 1886
> Liege (Montgomery), 1918
> Waterloo (once county seat of Clark), 1837
> Waterloo (Lafayette), about 1880

Spain:
> Alhambra (Stoddard), 1904
> De Soto (Jefferson), 1857
> Granada (Douglas), 1895
> Montserrat (Johnson), 1870
> New Madrid (city), 1788
> **NEW MADRID COUNTY**, 1812
> Ponce de Leon (Stone), 1882

Portugal:
> Lisbon (Howard), 1876

Italy:

Americus (Montgomery), 1869
Arcola (Dade), 1872
Columbus (Johnson), 1836
Como (New Madrid), 1879
Herculaneum (Jefferson), 1808
Lodi (Wayne), 1893
Milan (county seat of Sullivan), 1845
Modena (Mercer), 1856
Parma (New Madrid), 1903
Rome (Douglas), 1860
Taneycomo (Taney), 1914 (in part)
Venice (Shannon), 1915
Verona (Lawrence), 1868

Napoleon's shadow on the map of Missouri is attested by an amazing number of place names which exemplify the admiration many Missourians have felt for that able but ruthless military genius who so nearly conquered the world. The oldest of these Napoleonic names was *St. Helena,* so baptized for the island of his last exile. Once county seat of Pettis, it has dwindled now to a few ruined houses and shortened its name to *Helena.* But *Longwood,* six miles away, named for the island home in which he died, carries on its memories.

Napoleon's own name was honored in the adjoining county of Lafayette in 1836, whereupon, perhaps to hold the balance even, *Wellington* was founded five miles to the east, in 1837. Later on, in the '80s, arose the town of *Waterloo,* just halfway between them. An earlier *Waterloo* was the county seat of Clark from 1837 to 1871. It is said to have been named by an old French soldier who had fought in the famous battle.

Napoleon's name was also used for an imaginary town by Mark Twain in 1873. When he so named the metropolis of Marion County in his *Gilded Age,* he was smiling perhaps at the pretensions of *Marion City,* just as Dickens had already smiled at *Hannibal* in his *Martin Chuzzlewit* by calling it *New Thermopylae.* Two of his astonishing victories are called to mind by the names of *Arcola* and *Lodi.* And as *St. Helena* was the first, so *Elba,* the place of his earlier exile, was the last of the Napoleonic names to find a place in 1889 on the Missouri map.

The story of how what has been called the "Napoleonic Legend" suddenly arose about 1830, after he had been almost forgotten for a while, would require a volume. That legend flourished in America almost as mightily as it did in France. Six other States besides Missouri acquired towns named St. Helena; and there are 7 Napoleons, 10 Longwoods, 12 Elbas, 13 Wellingtons, 15 Lodis, and 24 Waterloos. But for some reason, no other State seems to have taken quite such a deep romantic interest in the dead dictator as did Missouri.

When the War of 1870 came between France and Germany, the sympathies of Missourians were mostly on the side of France, as is evidenced in the place names of *Metz, Urich,* and *Strasburg* adopted at about that time. *Urich* in Henry County was named for the French General Uhrich (1802-1886), who so heroically defended Strasburg against the Prussians. Still later, in 1918 during the first World War, the thoughts of all Missourians turned to the new French battlefields on which our own soldiers were fighting, and the names of *Argonne* and *Liege* were appropriated to our use.

Names from old Spain are surprisingly few, in view of the fact that, as we have seen above, names from New Spain are so extraordinarily numerous. We have honored two of Spain's remarkable explorers, De Soto and Ponce de Leon; and we have done the same for the two greatest of Italian discoverers, Christopher Columbus and Americus Vespucius, impartially providing one town for each of them.

NAMES FROM TEUTONIC AND SLAVIC COUNTRIES (41)

Germany: (and some Germans)

Altenberg (Perry), 1839
Baden (St. Louis), 1862
Berlin (Lafayette) about 1860
Bismarck (St. Francois), 1868
Bremen (St. Louis), 1850
Coelleda (Camden), about 1875
Dissen (Franklin), 1899
Dresden (Perry), 1839
Dresden (Pettis), 1876
Duden's Hill (Warren), 1827
Dutzow (Warren), 1835
Frankfort (Webster), 1858
Freistatt (Lawrence), 1873
Friedheim (Cape Girardeau), 1887
Frohna (Perry), 1839
Hamburg (St. Charles), 1841
Hanover (Jefferson), 1868
Hermann (Gasconade), 1837
Holstein (Warren), 1867
Kehl (Ste. Genevieve)
Koch (St. Louis), 1915
Mindenmines (Barton), 1883
New Melle (St. Charles), about 1850
Tilsit (Cape Girardeau), 1889
Weingarten (Ste. Genevieve), 1887
Westphalia (Osage), 1835
Wittenberg (Perry), 1839
Zell (Ste. Genevieve), 1886

Austria-Hungary:
> **Budapest** (Ripley), 1910
> **Vienna** (county seat of Maries), about 1855
> **Wien** (Chariton), 1877

Holland:
> **Amsterdam** (Bates), 1891
> **Wilhelmina** (Dunklin) 1915

Sweden:
> **Linneus** (Linn), 1840

Poland:
> **Krakow** (Franklin), 1870
> **Warsaw** (county seat of Benton), 1838

Serbia:
> **Belgrade** (Washington), 1876

Russia:
> **Moscow Mills** (Lincoln), 1821
> **Odessa** (Lafayette), 1878
> **Plevna** (Knox), 1877
> **Riga** (Ripley)

It is not surprising, to anyone who is familiar with the tremendous part played by our German-Americans in the making of Missouri, to discover that Germany has contributed more place names to our State than has any other country. The Germans came comparatively late, after the Indians, the French, and the American pioneers had successively occupied the land and had already named all the conspicuous features of the landscape and the oldest settlements. Before 1820, it is doubtful whether there was a single German of European birth in all of Missouri. But once they had arrived, they soon became a formative force, both by their numbers and by their character, in the life of the State; and it was not long before they set their stamp upon its place names as well.

The first German ever to settle in Missouri—at least the first with a university education—was that remarkable man Gottfried Duden. Born in 1785, in the Rhine Province of Germany, and educated at Goettingen, he came out to Missouri in 1824, bought a tract of land in what is now Warren County near Dutzow, where his name is still preserved at *Duden's Hill,* and remained for three years. In 1827 he returned to Germany, and in 1829 published his famous book, *Bereicht ueber eine Reise nach den westlichen Staaten Nordamerikas,* which at once became a best-seller and aroused wild enthusiasm among all classes in his native land for immediate emigration to the earthly paradise which he described in such glowing colors.

Missouri has never had a more ardent admirer than Duden. He waxed almost lyrical over his discovery of our Missouri pecans, persimmons, and pawpaws, and over the low prices of both land and living. He strenuously maintained that all the previous stories current in Germany about the perils of Western life—about prairie fires, hostile Indians, beasts of prey, poisonous serpents, and deadly diseases—were completely unfounded. Above all he praised our wonderful Missouri climate, particularly our Missouri autumns. "The great fertility of the soil, its enormous expanse, the splendid waterways, the absolute freedom of intercourse and safety of person and property, the very low rate of taxation—in what other country on earth are all these things combined?"

It was not, of course, Duden's rosy picture alone that sent the Germans streaming across the Atlantic during the next three decades. Widespread unrest and dissatisfaction with conditions in their own land, political, religious, and economic, drove many thousands of the finest people in Germany to abandon their birthplace and seek the liberty and the prosperity they could no longer find at home. But these loyal and liberty-loving Germans who came to Missouri never forgot their beloved Fatherland. Nor did they forget the names of the old German homes they had left behind them.

Among the many chapters of Missouri history written by the incoming Germans, the most dramatic is the story of the so-called "Saxon Migration" by German Lutherans to Perry County in 1839. Led by that strange and tragic character Bishop Martin Stephan (1777-1846), whose downfall and disgrace has been told and retold in a flood of books and controversial pamphlets, they finally succeeded in overcoming almost incredible difficulties, in holding fast to their beloved faith and church, in founding a remarkable institution of higher learning later to be known as *Concordia Seminary*, and at last in establishing their Perry County colony on a firm foundation. Four of their settlements at least received names from their homeland—*Altenberg, Wittenberg, Dresden,* and *Frohna*—though all of them have remained small except *Altenberg,* and one of them, *Dresden,* has entirely disappeared, to be replaced by another *Dresden* in Pettis County.

Among other famous Germans whose names are remembered in our Missouri place names are *Hermann,* better known to most of us by his Latinized name Arminius, (17 B.C.-21 A.D.) who saved the ancient Germans from enslavement by the Romans by decisively defeating them in the Teutoberg Forest in the year 9 A. D.; *Bismarck* (Prince Otto von Bismarck, 1815-1898), first Chancellor of the German Empire; and *Koch,* named for the Koch Hospital near by, which commemorates the celebrated German physician and bacteriologist Robert Koch (1843-1910).

Other distinguished foreigners honored by names of places in Missouri are Linnaeus (Karl von Linne, 1707-1778) of Sweden, the greatest botanist of his age, and *Wilhelmina* of Holland, Queen of the Netherlands from 1890 to 1948. The town of *Linneus* in Linn County, as we shall see, honored the great Swede more by afterthought than by original intention.

NAMES FROM AFRICA AND ASIA (12)

Africa:

Carthage (Jasper), 1842
Congo (Shannon), 1896
Dongola (Bollinger), 1900
Kimberly (Randolph), 1901
Oran (Scott), 1882
Tripoli (Newton)

India:

Cabool (Texas), 1882
Delhi (Crawford), 1886
Punjaub (Ste. Genevieve), 1867

Australia:

Melbourne (Harrison), 1897

Japan:

Japan (Franklin), 1860
Osaka (Taney), 1908

These far-flung names were adopted for various reasons: *Dongola* because it was much in the news in the '90s, in the war then being waged by England against the Mahdi; *Congo* because the postmaster had been studying the geography of Africa and was attracted by the name of its great river; *Cabool* for the capital of Afghanistan (now usually spelled Cabul or Kabul) and *Delhi* by real estate promotors who just liked the sound of them; *Kimberly*, a mining settlement accidentally misspelled for Kimberley, South Africa, which had attained world-wide note from its diamond-mine boom a few decades earlier; *Tripoli* because it has large deposits of magnesian limestone of the same quality as those exported from Tripoli in North Africa; and *Oran*, named by a retired sea-captain who had once visited the city in Algeria.

The little village of *Japan* came into considerable publicity after the Japanese attacked us at Pearl Harbor, and some Missourians began an agitation to change its name. It turned out that few of its inhabitants were aware of its connection with the enemy country, for down there the name is customarily pronounced as "JAY-pan" or "JAY-puhn," ('dʒɛ͵pæn or 'dʒepən) with the accent on the first syllable. The patriotic zeal of the agitators was further checked when the history of the name was brought to light. The village was really named, not for the country at all, but for the old Catholic Church there which has been in existence for more than a century. The "Church of the Holy Martyrs of Japan," to give its title in full, was named for the twenty-six priests and lay brothers of Spanish, Portuguese, and Japanese blood who were crucified for their faith on Feb. 5, 1597, in the great persecution that almost wiped out Japanese Christianity for the next three hundred years. When the pastor told its heroic story, the community decided to keep its name, which commemorated not only the savagery of the Japanese persecutors, but also the Japanese capacity for becoming saints and martyrs.

"Stay at home in Missouri and see the world!" is a popular slogan for which a strong case can be made out of our place names. A world tour may easily be taken without setting foot outside the confines of our State. All the important cities of Europe, Africa, Asia, and South America have been relocated within our borders, and have thriven well among us. And even if the ravages of war should ever reach our own land, and wipe out all the other forty-seven states, we should still have their most interesting American towns and cities quite safely domiciled somewhere in Missouri. Truly we could adapt Defoe's trenchant lines about his beloved England and describe Missouri as

> A State so various that it seems to be
> Not one, but all mankind's epitome.

B. HISTORICAL NAMES (455)

The borrowed names are particularly significant for the places from which they came. The historical and political names have their chief significance in the time when they were taken. When the dates and circumstances of their adoption or coinage are kept in mind, we have in them a surprisingly complete index to the history of Missouri, all the way down from its very earliest days. Our teachers of history might well find the best of all textbooks for their subject, if properly interpreted, to be the map of the State. As a matter of fact, if all other textbooks were lost entirely, we could recover most of its recorded history by studying our place names—and also a good deal of its history that has never been recorded.

INDIAN NAMES (94)

The oldest part of our history is naturally that of the Indian period, before the white man had set foot upon our soil. Nearly a hundred Indian names have been left behind for us to puzzle over—if we include not only those bequeathed to us from the many and various Indian tongues once spoken in the territory that is now Missouri, but also the translations and adaptations, often inaccurate or misunderstood, of their names into French or English, and the place names later coined by the whites from the tribal names or those of Indian personages or from the objects associated with the Indians.

The earliest dates of these Indian names are often highly uncertain, being merely the oldest surviving record of names which we know to have been far older. Dates have accordingly been omitted for all those we have reason to believe were in existence before 1800. Names no longer on the map have been starred in the index.

Abo (McDonald), 1886
Abo (Laclede), 1891
Arrow Rock (Saline), 1833
Black Hawk (Clark), 1833
Black Hawk Spring (Lincoln), 1815
Bon Homme Creek (St. Louis)
Bonne Femme Creek, Big (Randolph and Howard)
Bonne Femme Creek, Little (Callaway)
Calumet Creek (Pike)
Capaha Village (New Madrid)
Cent Deux (Andrew and Nodaway) before 1847 (French name
    for the One Hundred and Two River)
Chaonia (Wayne), 1887
Chilliticaux (Cape Girardeau)
Cote Sans Dessein (Callaway)
Des Arc (Iron), 1871
Des Moines River (Clark)
Femme Osage Creek (Warren and St. Charles)

Hahatonka (Camden), 1897
Hi Wassie (Oregon), 1867
Hoozaw River (Warren and St. Charles)
Huzzah Creek (Crawford)
Iatan (Platte), 1842
Illinois Road (St. Louis to Pemiscot)
Iowa (State)
Kahoka (Clark), 1867
Kansas (State)
Kansas City (Jackson), 1838
Kaw River (Jackson)
Kawsmouth (Jackson)
Kentucky (State)
Low Wassie Creek (Oregon), 1867
Marais Temps Clair (St. Charles)
Marmaton River (Bates and Vernon), 1839
Medoc (Jasper), before 1856
Mendota (Putnam), before 1873
Meramec River (Franklin and St. Louis)
Miami (Saline), 1843
Mineola (Montgomery), 1879
Mingo Bottoms (Bollinger), about 1834
Mississippi River
MISSISSIPPI COUNTY, 1845
Missouri River
Missouri (State)
Missouri City (Clay), 1859
Missouriton (St. Charles)
MONITEAU COUNTY, 1845
Moniteau Creek (Moniteau)
Montauk (Dent), 1860
"Mound City" (St. Louis)
Mound City (Holt), 1872
Neongwah River (Camden)
Neosho River (Newton)
Ne Ska River (New Madrid and Pemiscot)
Niangua River (Camden)
NIANGUA COUNTY, 1841 (later Dallas County)
Nishnabotna River (Atchison)
Nodaway River (Nodaway)
NODAWAY COUNTY, 1845
Ohaha River (Ralls to Pike)—now the Salt River
Ojibway (Wayne), 1888
Okaw (Kansas)
Oklahoma (State)
One Hundred and Two River (Andrew and Nodaway)
OREGON COUNTY, 1845
Osage River
OSAGE COUNTY, 1841
Osceola (St. Clair), 1836
Owasco (Sullivan), 1855

Ozark Mountains
OZARK COUNTY, 1841
Pemiscot Bayou (Pemiscot)
PEMISCOT COUNTY, 1851
Pocahontas (Cape Girardeau), 1855
"Poky Moonshine" (Franklin)
Portage des Sioux (St. Charles)
Puxico (Stoddard), 1887
Roche Perce Creek (Boone)
Sarcoxie (Jasper), 1833
Seneca (Newton), 1833
Shawnee (Jackson), 1832 (now Westport)
Tarkio (Atchison)
Taum Sauk Mountain (Iron)
Tecumseh (Ozark), 1898
Tywappity Bottoms (Scott)
Wakenda Creek (Carroll)
WAKENDA COUNTY, 1833 (first name proposed for Carroll)
Wakenda (Carroll), 1869
Wappapello (Wayne), 1884
Wasola (Ozark), 1912
Weaubleau Creek (Hickory)
Whosau Trace (Warren and St. Charles)
Wyaconda River (Scotland and Lewis)
Wyaconda (Scotland), 1853
Zewapeta (Scott)

Nine Missouri counties have Indian names, if we count *Oregon*, which was borrowed from the Far West, and the earlier names suggested for *Dallas* and *Carroll*, which were *Niangua* and *Wakenda*. They are all transfers from natural features, streams or mountains, which are almost always the first objects to be named.

Many different nations of red men lived and fought each other within the borders of Missouri, speaking entirely different languages. Missouri is notable as the meeting-place of the two greatest families of Indian tribes in all North America, the Algonquins and the Sioux. The languages of these two distinct confederacies were mutually unintelligible, being as much unlike each other as English is to Arabic or Chinese. To the Sioux, who came first, belong the closely related Osage, Missouri, Kansas, Iowa, and Arkansas or Quapaw tribes, among many others. All of them have left their names behind them. The Osage, most important of all, pronounced their own name as something like Wa-zha-zhe, which the white man turned into *Hoozaw, Huzzah,* or *Whosau* until the French made the more mellifluous *Osage* out of it. The Kansas tribe appears also as the *Kaw* or, with the French *aux* prefixed, the *Okaw;* and the Arkansas, by way of "aux Arks," have come down to us in the form *Ozarks,* and in the name of the town of

Des Arc (for Des Arcs). The Quapaw appear as *Capaha*. The general name of the confederacy appears in the name *Portage des Sioux*.

The alien Algonquins, who began to pour across the Mississippi only in the latter part of the Eighteenth Century, included the Delawares, Kickapoos, Shawnees, Moingonas (from whom *Des Moines* gets its name), possibly also the Illinois and their subdivision the Cahokians (hence the name *Kahoka*), and above all the Sauks and Foxes. They almost annihilated the Missouris, who had once been the most warlike of all the Sioux, and nearly caused their rightful name to be forgotten altogether. Missouri is the name their enemies knew them by; the Missouris called themselves the Niutachi, which probably meant "People Who Dwell at the Mouth of the River." *Portage des Sioux* traditionally marks the spot on the Mississippi where the defeated Sioux barely escaped their deadly foes, who were lying in wait for them at the mouth of the Missouri, by carrying their "big canoes" across country and getting away south of the Missouri.

It was the Fox who later on gave the white man more trouble than any other tribe, and perhaps for that reason left him the most important of all Indian place names, the *Mississippi* and the *Missouri*. The great *Mississippi* itself is the Fox *mesisi-piya*, meaning "Big River"—not, as is so often romantically affirmed, "Father of Waters." *Missouri* uses the same Fox prefix, and as we have seen probably signifies "Big-Canoe People." The name *Pemiscot* has the Fox prefix *pem-*, which means "by or alongside of," plus *-eskaw*, to "go or run," hence a body of water that runs alongside of another, a side-channel, which was a good name for *Pemiscot Bayou*. *Taum Sauk*, the highest mountain in Missouri, surely contains the name of the Sauk tribe, though what the significance of its first part may be remains a mystery.

The absolute difference in language between these two great confederacies is well illustrated by their respective words for God or the Great Spirit. All the Algonquins called Him Manito, Manitou, or some closely related term. The name for Him used by the Sioux, on the other hand, was Wakenda, Wakonda, or Wyaconda. Both names appear on the map of Missouri, apparently used first for rivers where the colonists found images of the Indian God carved or painted on the rocks at their mouths. Manito, in the French spelling *Moniteau*, was applied first to the two *Moniteau Creeks*, then to the county. *Wakenda*, for *Wakenda Creek*, was the first suggestion made for the name of Carroll County, and appears in Scotland County as *Wyaconda*. The Missourians ought to be a deeply religious people, with the Divine Name so widely spread over their map.

Again, the Fox word for "river," as we have seen, was *piya*, put at the end of river names, whereas the Siouan term was *ni* or *ne*, placed at the beginning. The Siouan name for the *Mississippi* was *Ni-tonga*, or "Big River," and for the Missouri *Ni-shodse,* or "Muddy River." Their names did not prevail for either of these, but they have come down to us in the names of many other streams and nearby places, such as *Neosho,* ("Main River"), *Ne Ska* or *Niska* ("White River"), *Nebraska* ("Flat River"), probably also in the *Niangua* or *Neongwah*—though we have not yet solved the full secret of that name.

There are three other interesting Osage words that may have left place-name children behind them, though in almost unrecognizable forms. These are the names traditionally handed down for their three ancestral villages, in which they were wont to take refuge in time of disastrous floods: Paçi, meaning Hilltop; Çondse, meaning Upland Forest; and Waxaga, meaning Thorny Thicket. If there is merit in a rather daring conjecture that has recently occurred to me, the first of these has survived to us in the Boone County stream which the French called the *Roche Percée* or *Rocher Percé,* and we call *Perche Creek* and pronounce today as the "PUHR shi" ('pɜˈʃɪ). The second Çondse, was twisted by the French into *Côte Sans Dessein* in Callaway County, and later on, by another French popular etymology, into *Cent Deux* river in Nodaway, rendered by their American successors as the *One Hundred and Two.* The third may provide the missing clue to the origin of the *Ohaha River* in Ralls and Pike Counties, now known as *Salt River.*[1]

We have also found an Osage explanation for those curious names for streams, the *Bon Homme, Bonne Femme,* and *Femme Osage.* We know that the topmost place in Osage society was held by the dignitary they called Nika-donhe, which signifies "Good Man." He it was who presided over the religious rites of the tribe, and it was his wife, the "Good Woman," who led the Indian women in their Dance of Peace and their agricultural ceremonies. It does not seem too much to assume that all these ancient streams took their names from highly respected and venerable chieftains and priestesses who once resided upon their banks. Two objects used in their rites have also provided us with place names: the calumet employed in their most sacred dance in *Calumet Creek,* and the funeral mounds, of which hundreds have been found in the State, in the sobriquet *Mound City* often used for St. Louis and in *Mound City* in Holt County.

Many other tribes of Indians, unrelated to either the Algonquin or the Sioux families, were driven to stay for a time in Missouri, and have left their names behind them: *Meramec, Miami,* Modoc (at *Medoc*), *Montauk, Ojibway, Seneca,* and Cherokee. The last named of these tribes, the Cherokees, one of the most remarkable of all Indian nations, only touched out

---

1 See the *Columbia Missourian,* Dec. 6, 1951, for a fuller presentation of this venturesome theory.

southern border for a year or two, and we should not be certain that they ever entered Missouri at all if it were not for two characteristic place names they left behind in Oregon County. They were driven from their ancient home in North and South Carolina and Georgia about 1800, and finally made their way through Tennessee into Arkansas some 16 or 18 years later. Among them was Sequoya, perhaps the most gifted man ever produced by the Indian race, who invented the Cherokee alphabet, and whom our botanists have honored by naming for him the biggest and oldest genus of trees found anywhere on our planet, the California redwood. Their language had a word *ayuhwasi,* meaning meadow or savannah. That word survives in the name of Hiwassee in Cherokee County, North Carolina, and also in Hiwassee River in Tennessee. We know they made incursions into Missouri in 1818 and 1819, but we could not be sure they stayed long enough to make settlements if it were not for the village of *Hi Wassie,* oldest place name in the county. The name *Low Wassie* for a nearby creek doubtless arose somewhat later, from a misinterpretation by white settlers of the true meaning of the Cherokee name.

The names of well known Indian personages have also been freely used for places: the chieftains *Osceola, Mingo, Iatan, Chaonia, Sarcoxie, Puxico, Wappapello,* and *Tecumseh,* and the famous Indian princess *Pocahontas.* The name of one Kickapoo chief has been handed down only in the French rendering Temps Clair, used for the lake in St. Charles known as *Marais Temps Clair;* and another still more famous, *Black Hawk,* only in an English version.

Often has the white man altered or twisted in strange ways the Indian names which he misunderstood or found difficult to pronounce, as in the cases already mentioned, if my conjectures are correct, of *Cent Deux* and *Sans Dessein* from Indian Çondse and *Percé* or *Perché* out of Paçi. In the name *Des Moines* the French made monks out of those wild warriors the Moingonas; they shortened Kansas to *Kaw,* or *Okaw,* and Arkansas to Arc, as in *Des Arc* and *Ozarks.* "Poky Moonshine" in Franklin County, used for a beautiful stretch of the Meramec, is just a fanciful transformation of Algonquian Pohquimoosi which had the prosaic sense of "place where the rocks are smoothly broken off." Often the white man simply made up an Indian sounding name which actually means nothing at all, as he seems to have done in *Hahatonka, Mendota, Mineola, Owasco,* and *Wasola.*

These intriguing Indian names have taken what may seem a disproportionate amount of our limited space, but it would require volumes to exhaust the many problems they present. Only the fringes of a few of these fascinating problems have here been touched upon. Unsolved as yet are the puzzles over the origin and significance of *Taum Sauk Mountain* and the *Niangua* or *Neongwah River,* of *Abo* and *Weaubleau, Tarkio* and *Chil-*

liticaux, of the *Marmaton,* the *Nishnabotna,* and the *Nodaway,* and oddest of all, of the name of old *Tywappity* or *Zewapeta* (which must surely be the same) *Bottoms* down in Scott County.

FRENCH AND SPANISH NAMES (114)

The French and Spanish names that have come down to us number more than a hundred. They include eleven of Missouri's counties. A large proportion of them are rivers, or are derived from the names of neighboring streams. Dates are often uncertain, and as in the case of the early Indian names have usually been omitted when earlier than 1800. When the French name has been translated into English or altered in its spelling by the later American inhabitants, the probable French original is added in parentheses.

Anse (or Ainse) a la Graisse (nickname for New Madrid)	
Auglaize Creek (Camden)	(Au Glaise)
Aux Vasse Creek (Callaway)	(Aux Vases)
Auxvasse (Callaway), after 1873	(Aux Vases)
Bellefontaine (St. Louis)	
Berger Creek (Franklin)	
Boeuf Creek (Franklin)	
Bois Brulé Creek (Cole)	
Bois d'Arc (Greene), 1878	
Bonne Terre (St. Francois), about 1825	
Bourbeuse River (Franklin)	
Brazeau Creek (Perry)	
Cabanne Course (St. Francois)	
Cabanne Place (St. Louis), 1877	
Cache River (Butler)	
Calvey Creek (Franklin)	(Calvé)
Cap au Gris (Lincoln), 1845	(Cap au Grès)
Cape Cinque Hommes (Perry)	(Cape St. Cosme)
Cape Girardeau, 1808	
CAPE GIRARDEAU COUNTY, 1812	
Carondelet (St. Louis)	
Cent Deux (Nodaway), before 1847	
Charette Creek (Warren)	(Chorette?)
Charrette (Warren)	
Chariton (Chariton), 1817	
CHARITON COUNTY, 1820	
Chemin du Roi (St. Louis to Pemiscot)	
Chouteau (Cole)	
Cooter (Pemiscot), 1854	(Coutre)
Cote Sans Dessein (Callaway)	
Courtois Creek (Washington)	
Courtois (Washington), 1886	
Creve Coeur Lake (St. Louis)	
Cuivre River (Lincoln)	
Current River (Dent, Shannon, Texas)	(Courante)
Dardenne Creek (Warren, St. Charles)	
Decypri (New Madrid), 1823	(Des Cyprès)

De Hodiamont (St. Louis)
De Lassus (St. Francois), 1870
Des Loge (St. Francois), 1893
De Soto (Jefferson) 1857
Des Peres River (St. Louis)
Dubois Creek (Franklin)
El Camino Real (St. Louis to Pemiscot)
Eleven Points River (Oregon)   (Pointes)
Fabius River (Marion, etc.)   (Fabiane?)
Florissant (St. Louis), 1785
Fort San Juan del Misuri (above St. Charles)
Fourche Creek (Ripley)
Fourche a Renault (Washington)
Flat River (St. Francois)   (Platte)
Gayoso (Pemiscot) 1851
Glaize Creek (Camden)
Gravois Creek (St. Louis)
Isle au Bois Creek (Jefferson)
Joachim Creek (Jefferson)
King's Highway (St. Louis to Pemiscot)   (Chemin du Roi)
Labadie (Franklin), 1855
LACLEDE COUNTY, 1845
Laclede (Linn,) 1853
Lamine River (Cooper)
Las Salinas (Ste. Genevieve)
Les Mamelles (St. Charles)
Lorimier's Ferry (Cape Girardeau), 1805
Loutre Island (Warren and Montgomery)
Luziere Creek (St. Francois), before 1870
Marais des Cygnes River (Bates), 1838
MARIES COUNTY, 1855   (Marais)
Marmaton River (Bates, Vernon), before 1839
Maupin Creek (Franklin)
Mine La Motte (Madison)
Misere (nickname for Ste. Genevieve)
NEW MADRID COUNTY, 1812
Nouvelle Madrid, 1789
Nuevo Madrid, 1788
Obrazo Creek (Perry)   (Au Brazeau)
Paincourt (nickname for St. Louis)
Papin (Jefferson)
Papinsville (Bates), 1847
Peruque Creek (Warren)
Platte River (Nodaway to Platte)
PLATTE COUNTY, 1828
Platte City (Platte), 1828
Pomme de Terre River (Polk)
Portage des Sioux (St. Charles)
Portageville (New Madrid), 1807
Rio Corrente (Current River)
Riviere Aux Vases (Ste. Genevieve)

Riviere Courante (Current River)
Roche Percée, or Rocher Perce (Boone), now called
    Perche Creek
Rocheport (Boone), 1825
Roubidoux (Texas), 1860
St. Charles, 1769
ST. CHARLES COUNTY, 1812
Ste. Genevieve, 1735
STE. GENEVIEVE COUNTY, 1812
St. Francois River (St. Francois to Butler)
ST. FRANCOIS COUNTY, 1821
St. John's Creek (Franklin)
St. Joseph (Buchanan), 1840
St. Louis, 1764
ST. LOUIS COUNTY, 1812
Salcedo (Scott), 1895
SALINE COUNTY, 1820

Sni or Sny (Lafayette), 1878	(Chenal)
Sniabar Creek (Lafayette)	(Chenal Hubert?)
Snicarty (Lewis)	(Chenal Écarté)
Swashin Creek (Jefferson)	(Joachim)
Tabo Creek (Lafayette)	(Tabeau or Thibeault)
Toad-a-Loop (Jackson)	(Tour de Loup)
Tour-de-Loup (Jackson)	
Vallés Mines (Jefferson), 1804	
Vide Poche (nickname for Carondelet)	
Zile au Boy Creek (Jefferson)	(Aux Isles au Bois)

The Spanish names are very few. Though under Spanish dominion for thirty-seven years (1763-1800), Missouri received no deep linguistic impression from Spain at that time. The extensive Spanish influence, as we have seen above, came later with the flood of Spanish place names borrowed mostly from New Spain in America. Three of the original counties were first organized and named by the Spanish: *St. Charles, New Madrid,* and *Cape Girardeau.* Several of the present names are translated from earlier French and these from still earlier Spanish names: so

> *New Madrid—Nouvelle Madrid—Nuevo Madrid*
> *King's Highway—Chemin du Roi—El Camino Real*
> *St. John—Saint Jean—San Juan*
> *Current River—Rivière Courante—Rio Corrente*

Spanish personal names are preserved in *De Soto, Gayoso,* and *Salcedo.* The only place name still used in its original Spanish form is *Las Salinas* ("The Salt Springs") in Ste. Genevieve County.

    Two names were borrowed: *New Madrid,* named *Nuevo Madrid* by Col. George Morgan in 1788 when he founded the city, in honor of the Spanish capital; and *Crève Coeur Lake,* probably named as we have seen above for Crève Coeur Fort in Illinois, which was so named by La Salle for the Dutch fortress Crèvecoeur in honor of its capture by his royal master Louis XIV. Six saints have been honored—Charles, Francis, Genevieve, John, Joseph, and Louis—with intentions and implications that will be discussed later on, along with other cultural and religious names.

All the remaining French names fall into two nearly equal classes, descriptive and personal. The descriptive names were conferred for the landscape, flora or fauna, or other natural features. The precise meaning of the French terms used in these descriptive names needs fuller explanation.[1]

Anse or Ainse: a cove or little bay
Anse à la Graisse: Grease Cove, i.e. one abounding in tallow or bear's fat
Auglaize and Glaize: *glaise,* meaning clay or lick for wild beasts
Aux Vases: swamps or morasses
Bellefontaine: beautiful spring or fountain
Boeuf: for *boeuf sauvage,* buffalo
Bois Brulé: burnt wood, sometimes used for a half-breed
Bois d'Arc: bow-wood, now popularly known as the "Osage orange"
Bonne Terre: good land, especially for mining; rich in ore
Bourbeuse: muddy
Cache: place of deposit, or buried stores
Cap au Gris: for *grès,* sandstone
Cent Deux: 102, the French name used before 1847 for the One Hundred
    and Two River. See above for the conjecture that it was a popular
    etymology for Osage Çondse, upland forest.
Côte Sans Dessein: a hill "without purpose." McDermott thinks it might
    have been used of a hill so located that there seems no purpose or reason
    for it to be there, one cut off from the other hills or bluffs that one would
    ordinarily expect to find with it. But see above for the conjecture that
    this too was just a popular etymology for Osage Çondse, upland forest.
Cuivre River: an unsolved puzzle. The word of course means copper, but
    there are no traces of copper in the vicinity. The French may of course
    have been misled by false reports, or there may be another hidden
    "popular etymology" behind the name.
Crève Coeur Lake: used for a fort that was thought to be a "heart-breaker,"
    not to be captured easily.
Current River: from French *Courante,* running swiftly.
Decypri: for *Des Cyprès,* the red cedar, or the grey pine.
Eleven Points: in Mississippi Valley French, *pointe* meant a wooded point
    of land—a contribution of the *voyageur* who measured distance on a
    river by the bends of the stream, as indicated by the points or arms
    protruding.
Florissant: prosperous. Missouri French for *Fleurissant.*
Fourche: fork of a river; creek.
Gravois: gravel.
Isle au Bois: a grove of trees on the open prairie or along a river bank.
    Zile au Boy must be from the plural form, Aux Isles au Bois.
Lamine or Mine: mine, particularly lead mine.

1 Due acknowledgment must be made here of information taken from the outstanding authority in this field, John Francis McDermott's *Glossary of Mississippi Valley French,* 1941.

Les Mamelles: hills or cone-shaped bluffs.

Loutre: otter.

Marais: marsh; more commonly used of a lake or pond.

Marais des Cygnes: swan-lake.

Marmaton: a scullion or cook. McDermott says the chief cook of an Osage village was a great dignitary, a sort of grand chamberlain. The river may have been named because one of these exalted officials lived on its banks. But it seems more likely to have been an Indian term, perhaps misunderstand and modified.

Misère: poverty. The jest signified that Ste. Genevieve was considered a place of little importance, or else that the land around it was barren.

Paincourt: short of bread, or suspected of selling bread that was short of weight. The jest implied, says McDermott, that St. Louis was commercial rather than agricultural.

Peruque: an unsolved puzzle. No plausible explanation of the wig has been found.

Platte: of a stream, shallow, low, apt to run dry.

Pomme de Terre: used of the cowberry, groundnut, or wild bean.

Portage: carrying a canoe and its load of freight from one navigable stretch of water to another.

Roche, or Rocher: stone, boulder; rock, crag, or cliff.

Roche Percée, or Rocher Percé: this apparently meant, as Captain Clark interpreted it in his *Journal,* a "split rock" or a pierced or perforated crag or cliff. The present pronunciation, however, which is always "PUR-shi," indicates that the name actually used by the French boatmen was Roche Perchée, i.e., a boulder perched or "roosting" on the top of the bank. For the possibility that either name was a mere popular etymology for Osage Paçi, hilltop, see above.

Saline: salt spring or lick.

Sni: for *chenal* or the dialect *chenail,* a channel.

Snicarty: for *chenal écarté,* a narrow channel, not the main channel of the river.

Tour-de-Loup: wolf-track

Vide Poche: empty pocket. The jest may have implied that the people of Carondelet often had empty pockets, are else that they had a habit of emptying the pockets of their visitors.

The personal names preserve the memory of a number of the most famous dignitaries and leading men of early French and Spanish days, as well as some of the humbler settlers.

Berger: probably for Joseph Berger, hunter, or for Pierre Berger, merchant of St. Louis, who died in 1787. The pronunciation with soft *g* shows that it cannot be, as is sometimes affirmed, for the well known German leader Caspar Burger.

Brazeau, and Obrazo: Joseph Brazeau, a St. Louis merchant from 1791 to 1799, or some other member of his important family.

Cabanne: a well known old family of St. Louis.

Calvey Creek: Joseph Calvé, fur-trader, who came to St. Louis in 1765, or some other member of the Calvé family.

Cape St. Cosme: Father St. Cosme, of Quebec, who visited the spot in 1698.

Cape Girardeau: Ensign Sieur Girardeau (or Girardat), stationed at Kaskaskia 1704-1720, later a prosperous fur trader.

Charette, Charrette, Chariton: ?Joseph Chorette, St. Louis fur trader, who was drowned in the Missouri River in 1795; or possibly another trader named John (or Jean) Chariton.

Carondelet: Baron Francesco Luis Hector de Carondelet (1748-1807) Governor General of Louisiana.

Chouteau: Auguste Chouteau (1750-1829), clerk and chief lieutenant of Pierre Laclede at the founding of St. Louis; or some other member of his famous family.

Cooter: the Coutre family, one of whom was a merchant in New Madrid in 1795.

Courtois: an unidentified settler. The name is locally pronounced and sometimes written as Coataway or Cotoway.

Dardenne: the Dardenne family, early pioneers in the Mississippi Valley.

De Hodiamont: said to be named for Baron De Hodiamont, a Polish nobleman.

De Lassus, and also Luzière Creek: Don Carlos (Charles) de Lassus de Luzière, the last French Governor of Upper Louisiana, 1799-1804. After the Annexation, he turned the colony over to Captain Amos Stoddard, the first American Governor, and retired to New Orleans. His son Auguste came back to St. Louis in 1868, and spent his last years on his ancestral estate in St. Francois County.

Des Loge: Firmin Des Loge, of St. Francois, opened the mine here in 1875.

De Soto: Fernando De Soto (1500-1542), who discovered the Mississippi River in 1541.

Des Pères: the Fathers of some Catholic order, probably the Jesuits, who settled at the mouth of the river in 1700.

Dubois Creek: Louis Dubois, pioneer.

Fabius River: the earliest forms of the name are Fabiane (1809) and Ferbien (1822). He was probably some unidentified trapper or trader of early days in northeast Missouri.

Fourche à Renault: Philip Francois Renault received a grant to work the mines here in 1723.

Gayoso: Don Miguel Gayoso was Spanish Governor of Natchez in 1795.

Gratiot: Charles Gratiot (1752-1817) came from Switzerland to St. Louis about 1777.

Joachim: a common French family name. Locally pronounced and sometimes written Swashin or Swashing.

Labadie: Sylvestre Labaddie (or L'Abaddie), who came to St. Louis about 1769 and in 1776 married a daughter of the Chouteau family. He died in 1794. The Franklin County names are more probably for his even more prominent son, Sylvestre Labaddie, Jr. (1779-1849), an associate of other St. Louisians and of Governor William Clark in the famous American Fur Co.

Laclede: Pierre Laclede Liguest (1724-1778), founder of St. Louis in 1764.

Lorimier Ferry: Louis Lorimier (1748-1812), founder of Cape Girardeau in 1808.

Maupin: the Maupin family were early settlers.

Mine La Motte: Probably for Antoine de la Mothe Cadillac, founder of
Detroit in 1701, Governor General of Louisiana 1711-1717. He discovered the mines here in 1714.

Papin: Melicourt Papin was a prominent Indian trader.

Roubidoux: Joseph Roubidoux (1783-1886), trapper and explorer, who
founded St. Joseph in 1840 and named it for his patron saint.

Salcedo: Don Manuel de Salcedo was Spanish Governor of Texas in 1803.

Sniabar: Probably named for Antoine Hubert, St. Louis merchant, who
traded there 1768; or possibly for Francis Hébert (1750-1780), a well
known St. Louis landowner.[1]

Tabo: May have been named for Francis Thibaut or Tabeau, who received
grants of lots in St. Louis from Laclede in 1765; or perhaps for Charles
B. Thibeault, who settled at Cuivre in Lincoln County in 1799.

Vallés: The Vallé family came from Normandy to Quebec in 1645. Francois
Vallé, or his son, Don Francesco Vallé, opened the Jefferson County
mines about 1790.

NAMES FROM NATIONAL HISTORY (182)

Passing on from the Indian and the French and Spanish periods of
Missouri's growth, from the colonial to the strictly national part of our
history, we shall survey next the place names that reflect the passionate
interest always felt by Missourians in events taking place in the nation as a
whole, and in the men who made them. These national names fall naturally
into three sub-groups: places named for presidents and vice-presidents and
the rival aspirants for our topmost office, those named for other national
leaders and statesmen, and those named for our military leaders.

PRESIDENTIAL NAMES (84)

More than eighty Missouri place names fall into this group. They include the names of 20 of our counties: 11 named for presidents, 3 for vice-
presidents, and 6 for men who ran for the two highest offices without success, although many of them were distinctly preferred in Missouri to the
successful candidates. As for towns, the hampering rule of the Postal Department that no two post-offices may have precisely the same name has
been evaded in several ways: by using a man's first or middle name, his
popular sobriquet or nickname, or his home; also by compounding his name
with a variety of suffixes.

Missouri has always been a battleground at the time of our national
elections. It is a striking fact that places of more or less importance have
been named in our State for every one of our Presidents, with one single
exception, until after the election of Woodrow Wilson. The clearest way to
show this will perhaps be to list these place names by the presidential ad-
ministrations, prefacing each administration by the year of first election.

1 This derivation of Sniabar from Chenal Hubert or Chenal Hébert has been
discussed, with full presentation of the available evidence, in my *Introduction to a
Survey of Missouri Place Names,* 1934, pages 32-36.

1789: George Washington, with his home at Mount Vernon.

WASHINGTON COUNTY, 1813
Washington (Franklin), 1822
Georgetown (first county seat of Pettis), 1837
Washington Park (St. Louis), 1840
Mount Vernon (county seat of Lawrence), 1845
Washington University (St. Louis), 1854

It was highly appropriate that the very first new county to be organized, after the five original Spanish districts, should be named for the first President. The venerated name was next adopted for its largest town by the neighboring county to the west, which had to be content with calling itself *Franklin.* Previously the town of *Washington* had considered briefly the less inspiring names of *Owensville, Bassora,* or *Goosetown.* Then Pettis County, not to be outdone, named its first county seat *Georgetown,* using Washington's first name, an idea borrowed from Georgetown, Kentucky. Soon afterwards St. Louis decided to christen one of its most beautiful parks with Washington's name. In 1853, its great institution of higher learning was incorporated at first under the name of *Eliot Seminary,* in honor of its president William G. Eliot; but at the first board meeting on Feb. 22, 1854, Dr. Eliot modestly requested that the name be changed to *Washington University,* since it was Washington's birthday.

There was fierce rivalry for the name of Washington's home, the beloved Mount Vernon. Five Missouri towns wanted the name. The first to adopt it was old *Mount Vernon* in Lafayette County, which served as its earliest county seat from 1820 to 1822, when the coveted prize went to Lexington instead. A town in Moniteau was laid out with the name in 1836, and another in Gentry; and it was proposed in 1837 for the town that hoped to become county seat of Clark, only to be rejected in favor of *Waterloo.* After all these, for one reason or another, had failed to survive, the envied name went at last to the thriving town that in 1845 became the county seat of Lawrence.

We have in addition to the six names here listed 34 Washington Schools, 29 Washington Townships, and at least 7 Washington Churches, making a grand total of more than 70 places in the State honoring the memory of the Father of His Country.

1796: John Adams.

Adams School (St. Louis), 1878
Adams Township (De Kalb), 1870

Our second president was never well known nor very popular in Missouri. The State entered the Union after his administration was over, and after his old Federalist Party had fallen into disrepute. In contrast to the first and third presidents, there seem to be only two examples of the use of John Adams's name, both of minor importance.

1800: Thomas Jefferson, with his home at Monticello in Virginia.

> **JEFFERSON COUNTY,** 1818
> **Jefferson City** (State Capital), 1822
> **Jefferson Barracks** (St. Louis), 1826
> **Monticello** (county seat of Lewis), 1833
> **Hillsboro** (county seat of Jefferson), 1839

Jefferson County, next to be organized after Washington, and *Jefferson City,* our State Capital, were so named during Jefferson's lifetime, as a personal tribute to the man who made the Louisiana Purchase. The historic *Jefferson Barracks* honored him in the year of his death. His home at *Monticello* was eagerly vied for as well. Two Monticellos, one in Howard County in 1821 and another in Chariton in 1831, were laid out only to be swept away by the flood waters of the Missouri. Then in 1833, Lewis County stepped in and carried off the prize for its county seat, to the bitter disappointment of Jefferson County, which felt that its name somehow gave it a prescriptive right to *Monticello*. It was too late, however, and had to be content with a translation of the Italian name into its English equivalent Hillsboro. There are also 13 Jefferson Schools and 19 Jefferson Townships in Missouri, giving him a total of nearly 40 name-children, second only to Washington. He will always be regarded as our own particular President.

1808: James Madison, who defeated in 1812 the very popular De Witt Clinton, later Governor of New York and a prime mover in constructing the Erie Canal.

> **MADISON COUNTY,** 1818
> **CLINTON COUNTY,** 1833
> **Madison** (Monroe), 1836
> **Clinton** (county seat of Henry), 1836
> **Madisonville** (Mercer), 1856
> **Clintonville** (Cedar), 1857

1816: James Monroe.

> **MONROE COUNTY,** 1831
> **Monroe City** (Monroe), 1856

1824: John Quincy Adams. He defeated Andrew Jackson, who had won the Battle of New Orleans in 1815, Henry Clay, chief designer of the Missouri Compromise of 1820, and William Harris Crawford of Georgia, Senator and Cabinet Member. All three of his opponents were popular in Missouri, where Adams had only scattering support.

> **Jackson** (county seat of Cape Girardeau), 1815
> **CLAY COUNTY,** 1822
> **JACKSON COUNTY,** 1826

CRAWFORD COUNTY, 1829
Quincy (Hickory), 1848
Adams School (Kansas City)

1828: Andrew Jackson, known as "Old Hickory," with his home called "The Hermitage" at Nashville, Tennessee. He defeated Henry Clay in 1832 in Clay's second candidacy.

Jacksonville (Platte), 1830 (now New Market)
?ANDREW COUNTY, 1841
HICKORY COUNTY, 1845
Hermitage (county seat of Hickory), 1847
Jacksonville (Nodaway), 1856 (now extinct)

The county history maintains that *Andrew County* was named for Andrew Jackson Davis, a local lawyer, which seems doubtful. If so, it would make it for the President at one remove. Jackson is the only President who has three Missouri counties named for him. But the only surviving Jacksonville in the State, in Randolph County, was named for an early settler (see page 80). There are 7 Jackson Schools and 23 Jackson Townships, making a total of 36 places named for him, almost as many as for Jefferson. Clay had 7 schools and 16 townships named for him, at varying dates from 1825 to 1865.

1836: Martin Van Buren, whose home was at Kinderhook, New York. His Vice-President was Richard Mentor Johnson of Kentucky.

Van Buren (Carter), 1830
JOHNSON COUNTY, 1834
VAN BUREN COUNTY, 1835-1848 (now Cass County)
KINDERHOOK COUNTY, 1841-1843 (now Camden County)

The slogan of "Old Kinderhook," used by the supporters of Van Buren in these exciting campaigns, and its abbreviation in the letters "O.K.," was according to a plausible theory the true origin of what has been called the best known and most characteristic term in the American language. But Van Buren lost most of his popularity after his crushing defeat in 1840, and both the counties named for him changed their names.

1840: William Henry Harrison, the hero of Tippecanoe, and after his death his Vice-President John Tyler.

Tippecanoe (Schuyler), about 1840
Tyler Township (Polk), about 1840
Tyler Township (Hickory), 1845

There are 4 Harrison Schools and 6 Harrison Townships in the State.

1844: James Knox Polk of Tennessee. His Vice-President was George Mifflin Dallas of Pennsylvania. He defeated Henry Clay, whose home in

Lexington, Kentucky, was known as "Ashland," in Clay's third and last candidacy.

POLK COUNTY, 1835
DALLAS COUNTY, 1844
Dallas (county seat of Harrison), 1845 (now Bethany)
Claysville (Boone), 1844
Clay (Adair), about 1844
Clay Mansion (St. Louis), 1845
Ashland (Boone), 1853
Polktown (Polk), 1879

Polk was only a Congressman when *Polk County* was named for him, but was perhaps more popular then in Missouri than after his unexpected election to the Presidency ten years later. Henry Clay built *Clay Mansion* in 1845 on his estate "Old Orchard" near St. Louis, but may have lived there only a few months. He died at "Ashland" in 1852, and the Boone County town adopted the name the following year.

1848: Zachary Taylor, known as "Old Rough and Ready," and after his death in 1850 his Vice-President Millard Fillmore of New York. They defeated Lewis Cass and William Orlando Butler, Democratic candidates for President and Vice-President, whom most Missourians preferred.

Fillmore (Andrew), 1845
Cassville (Barry), 1845
CASS COUNTY, 1848
BUTLER COUNTY, 1849
Taylor Township (Shelby), 1849
Butler (Bates), 1852
"Rough and Ready School" (Buchanan)

There are also Taylor Townships in Adair and Grundy counties.

1852: Franklin Pierce, defeating General Winfield Scott, the Whig candidate. Daniel Webster of Marshfield, Massachusetts (1782-1852), was an unsuccessful candidate for the Whig nomination.

?Scottsville (Sullivan), 1847
Webster College (St. Louis), 1850
Pierce Township (Stone), 1853
WEBSTER COUNTY, 1855
Marshfield (county seat of Webster), 1855
Webster Groves (St. Louis), 1867

Eight Webster Schools likewise bear evidence of the greater regard felt for him in Missouri than for Pierce, his almost unknown but accidentally successful rival, or for General Scott.

1856: James Buchanan, defeating John Charles Fremont, the Republican candidate.

BUCHANAN COUNTY, 1839
Fremont (Cedar), 1847 (now Stockton)
Buchanan (Bollinger), 1886

Both men, as the dates indicate, were more popular before the election than after it. The Cedar County town was named for Fremont when he was famous as explorer and general, but it changed its name in 1857 when he became the Republican candidate. The present *Fremont* in Carter County was named in 1887 for another man (see page 117).

1860: Abraham Lincoln, defeating Stephen Arnold Douglas. Upon Lincoln's death in 1865 he was succeeded by Vice-President Andrew Johnson.

> **DOUGLAS COUNTY**, 1857
> **Johnson City** (St. Clair), 1867
> **Lincoln** (Benton), 1868
> **Lincolnville** (negro section of Sedalia), 1872

Very slowly did Lincoln overcome the far greater popularity of his rival Douglas in Missouri. Today, however, he is honored by the names of 24 Lincoln Schools (12 white and 12 colored) and 13 Lincoln Townships, giving him almost as many name-children in the State as Jefferson and Jackson.

1868: Ulysses Simpson Grant, whose log cabin near St. Louis where he lived from 1848 till 1859 during his early struggle with poverty was named by him "Hardscrabble."

> **Grant City** (county seat of Worth), 1863
> **Grantsville** (Linn), 1866
> **Grant** (Holt), 1869
> **Grant's Log Cabin** (St. Louis), a shrine since 1900

There are also 12 Grant Townships, 8 Grant Schools, and 4 Hardscrabble Schools in the State.

1876: Rutherford Birchard Hayes, defeating Samuel Jones Tilden.

> **Tilden** (Dallas), 1889
> **Hayes School** (Lincoln)

1880: James Abram Garfield. Upon his death in 1881 he was succeeded by Vice-President Chester Alan Arthur.

> **Garfield Park** at Washington (Franklin), 1881
> **Garfield** (Oregon), about 1885

It is just possible that the name *Chester*, suggested but not adopted in 1882 for the town in Miller County which has preferred to be called *Olean*, was meant for President Arthur. Otherwise Arthur is our only President before Harding whose name is entirely absent from the list of Missouri place names.

1884: Grover Cleveland, who was re-elected in 1892.

> **?Grover** (St. Louis), 1889-1904
> **Cleveland** (Cass), about 1900
> **Grover College** (Clark)

The school called *Grover College* was formerly known as *Jeff Davis School*, for Jefferson Davis, President of the Confederate States from 1861 to 1865.

1888: Benjamin Harrison.
Benjamin Harrison School (Kansas City)

1896: William McKinley. Upon his death in 1901 he was succeeded by Theodore Roosevelt, who was re-elected in 1904.
McKinley Bridge (St. Louis)
Roosevelt (Douglas), 1906

There are also 9 McKinley Schools, 2 McKinley Townships, and 2 Roosevelt Schools.

1908: William Howard Taft.
Taft (Butler), 1910

1912: Woodrow Wilson.
Woodrow Mine (Lafayette), about 1920
Wilson Township (Dallas), 1921

None of our later presidents has as yet had any places named for him, unless we count street-names. The present incumbent, who happens to be the first President born in Missouri, was recently honored by the name of *Truman Road* (formerly Fifteenth Street) in Kansas City.

OTHER NATIONAL LEADERS AND STATESMEN (34)

Among the great men of the nation, outside of Missouri, who never aspired to the presidential chair, there are twenty-two who have lent their names, directly or indirectly, to places in our State. Some of these names came to us indirectly, having been borrowed from other States that honored these men before us, in which cases the names have already been listed in the preceding section. One was a British statesman, who has always been regarded as one of ours because he warmly favored the cause of the Colonies before the Revolution. There are over thirty place names in this group, including the names of fourteen of our counties. These leaders have been arranged in chronological order.

Benjamin Franklin of Philadelphia (1706-1790).
Franklin (Howard), 1816 (now known as Old Franklin)
FRANKLIN COUNTY, 1818
New Franklin (Howard), 1828

More than 20 Franklin Schools and at least 5 Franklin Townships were named for him in Missouri. Over 50 places in other States bear his name.

Earl Camden (Charles Pratt) of England (1714-1794), leader of the Whig Party, and Chancellor of England from 1766 to 1770.
CAMDEN COUNTY, 1843 (the former Kinderhook County)
Camden (Ray), 1845
Camdenton (new county seat of Camden), 1930

Patrick Henry of Virginia (1736-1799).
HENRY COUNTY, 1841

Charles Carroll of Carrollton, Maryland (1737-1832).
CARROLL COUNTY, 1833
Carrollton (county seat of Carroll), 1833

Isaac Shelby of Kentucky (1750-1826), Governor of Kentucky, 1792-1806 and 1812-1816.
SHELBY COUNTY, 1835
Shelbyville (county seat of Shelby), 1836
Shelbina (Shelby), 1857

John Marshall of Virginia (1755-1835), Chief Justice of the U. S., 1801-1835.
Marshall (county seat of Saline), 1840

Alexander Hamilton of New York (1754-1804), Secretary of the Treasury, 1789-1795.
Hamilton (Caldwell), 1855
5 Hamilton Schools

Nathaniel Macon of North Carolina (1757-1837), Senator, 1816-1828.
MACON COUNTY, 1837
Macon (county seat of Macon), 1856

John Adair of Kentucky (1759-1840), Governor, 1820-1824.
ADAIR COUNTY, 1841

Albert Gallatin of Pennsylvania (1761-1849), Secretary of the Treasury, 1801-1814.
Gallatin (county seat of Daviess), 1837

Edward Livingston of New York (1764-1836), Secretary of State, 1831-33.
LIVINGSTON COUNTY, 1837

Robert Fulton of New York (1765-1815), who built our first steamboat in 1807.
Fulton (county seat of Callaway), 1822

John Randolph of Roanoke, Virginia (1773-1833), Senator and Congressman.
RANDOLPH COUNTY, 1829

Felix Grundy of Tennessee (1777-1840), Senator and Attorney General.
GRUNDY COUNTY, 1841

Roger Brooke Taney of Maryland (1777-1864), Chief Justice, 1836-1864. He decided the famous "Dred Scott Case" in 1857.
TANEY COUNTY, 1837
Taney Creek (Franklin), ab. 1865
Taneycomo (Taney), 1914

John Forsyth of Georgia (1780-1841), Secretary of State, 1834-1841.
    Forsyth (county seat of Taney), 1838

William Taylor Barry of Kentucky (1785-1835), Postmaster General under
    Jackson
    Barry (Clay), 1830
    BARRY COUNTY, 1835

William Cabell Rives of Virginia (1793-1868), Senator 1833-1845). He lost
    popularity in Missouri by turning Whig in 1835.
    RIVES COUNTY, 1835 (changed to Henry in 1841)

Silas Wright of New York (1795-1847), Senator, 1833-1844, and Governor,
    1845-1847.
    WRIGHT COUNTY, 1841

Mirabeau Buonaparte Lamar of Texas (1798-1859), President of Texas,
    1838-1841.
    Lamar (county seat of Barton), 1846

James Campbell of Pennsyvania (1812-1893), Postmaster General, 1852.
    Campbellton (Franklin), 1854

Daniel S. Appleton of New York City (1824-1890), head of Appleton Pub-
    lishing Company.
    Appleton City (St. Clair), 1872

NAMES FOR SOLDIERS AND SAILORS (64)

More than 60 places in the State, among them 30 of our counties, have
received military and naval names, which testify to the unbounded admiration felt by our pioneers and later settlers as well for more than 40 of our
leaders in war. If the names already listed of presidents and statesmen,
many of whom were of course equally distinguished as military leaders,
were included, and if we had space to add at least 50 schools and as many
townships, we could easily increase the total list of such names to well over
two hundred.

There has been a notable diminution, however, in these warlike names
as time went on. Since the Civil War, such names have almost become conspicuous by their absence. From 20 soldiers of the Revolution, there was a
decline to only 10 from the War of 1812 and the accompanying Indian
wars, 2 from the Mexican War and only 3 from all our later conflicts, together with 8 from our entire naval history.

SOLDIERS OF THE REVOLUTION (32)

Buncombe, Col. Edward, of North Carolina, who fought at Brandywine
and died in 1777 of wounds received at Germantown. Buncombe County,
N. C., was named for him in 1791. Had not the congressman from that dis-

trict, in the debate of 1820 over the Missouri Compromise, made the famous excuse for his long and tedious oratory by declaring that he was only "speaking for Buncombe," the name of this brave soldier would never have acquired the entirely undeserved implication that has since made our "bunkum" and "bunk" one of the most derogatory and familiar of all Americanisms. It does not seem to have carried any such unworthy implication as yet when it was adopted for at least the first two places that have employed it in Missouri.

Buncombe (Franklin), 1842
Buncomb Ridge (Ripley and Butler)
Buncombe (Pettis), 1870

De Kalb, Baron John, of Bavaria (1721-1780), who fell at Camden.
DE KALB COUNTY, 1845
De Kalb (Buchanan), 1851

Greene, Gen. Nathaniel, of Rhode Island (1742-1786).
GREENE COUNTY, 1833

Jasper, Sgt. William (1750-1779), who fell at Savannah.
JASPER COUNTY, 1841

Knox, Gen. Henry, of Boston (1750-1806): Washington's Chief of Artillery, and Secretary of War 1785-1794.
KNOX COUNTY, 1845

Lafayette, Marquis Jean Paul de, of France (1757-1834). He revisited the United States in 1824-1825).
Fayette (Howard), 1822
LAFAYETTE COUNTY, 1825

Lincoln, Gen. Benjamin, of Massachusetts (1733-1810). He was Secretary the War 1781-1783.
LINCOLN COUNTY, 1818

McDonald, Sergeant. A soldier of whom little could be discovered.
McDONALD COUNTY, 1849

Marion, Gen. Francis, of South Carolina (1732-1795); known as the "Swamp Fox."
Marion (first county seat of Cole), 1821-1829
MARION COUNTY, 1826
Marion College, 1831
Marionville (Lawrence), 1854

Mercer, Gen. Hugh (1721-1777), who fell at Princeton.
MERCER COUNTY, 1845

Montgomery, Gen. Richard (1736-1775), who fell at Quebec.
MONTGOMERY COUNTY, 1818
Montgomery City (Montgomery), 1853

Morgan, Gen. Daniel, of New Jersey (1736-1802).
  MORGAN COUNTY, 1833

Newton, Sgt. John. One of "Marion's men," with Sgt. Jasper.
  NEWTON COUNTY, 1838

Pulaski, Count Casimir, of Poland (1748-1779), who fell at Savannah.
  PULASKI COUNTY, 1833

Putnam, Gen. Israel, of Massachusetts (1718-1790).
  PUTNAM COUNTY, 1845

St. Clair, Gen Arthur (1734-1818), who was governor of the Northwest Territory 1789-1802.
  ST. CLAIR COUNTY, 1841

Schuyler, Gen. Philip, of New York (1733-1804), who was Indian Commissioner during the Revolutionary War.
  SCHUYLER COUNTY, 1843

Sullivan, Gen. John, of New Hampshire (1740-1795); member of the Continental Congress.
  SULLIVAN COUNTY, 1843

Warren, Gen. Joseph, of Massachusetts (1741-1775), who fell at Bunker Hill.
  WARREN COUNTY, 1833
  Warrenton (county seat of Warren), 1837
  Warren (Marion), 1853

Wayne, Gen. Anthony ("Mad Anthony"), of Pennsylvania, who commanded the Army of the West 1794-1796.
  WAYNE COUNTY, 1818
  Waynesville (county seat of Pulaski), 1839
  Wayne City (Jackson), 1847

Most of these Revolutionary names, as we have seen, had already been adopted in other States, particularly in Kentucky and Tennessee; and many of them were doubtless borrowed from these neighbors by Missourians, as we know to have been the case with *Lincoln County* from Kentucky and *Sullivan County* from Tennessee. At the same time, the adoration felt for all the Revolutionary leaders was extraordinarily strong in Missouri, even though our State was not yet a part of the Union when the War of Independence was fought. Next to General Washington, who of course leads all the rest, stands Marion with 15 name-children (if we count in all the schools and townships named for him), together with three of "Marion's Men": Sgt. Jasper with eight names, and Sgts. Newton and McDonald. Next in popularity were Warren, Wayne, and Greene. Our deep gratitude is likewise shown to three foreigners who came over to help us: De Kalb, Pulaski, and especially the beloved Lafayette. All three have left their names scattered right across the entire country. Lafayette has more than fifty places named for him outside of Missouri. It is noteworthy that the Marquis's name was first used in the shorter form of Fayette, and only later, after his visit of 1824-1825, began to take on the longer form of Lafayette.

WAR OF 1812, AND THE INDIAN WARS (12)

Caldwell, Matthew, commander of Indian Scouts in Kentucky.

CALDWELL COUNTY, 1836

Callaway, Capt. James (1783-1815), grandson of Boone, who fell in battle with the Indians.

CALLAWAY COUNTY, 1820

Cole, Capt. Stephen, who came from Virginia to Missouri in 1807, and died in 1822.

COLE COUNTY, 1820

Dade, Capt. Francis L., from Virginia, who was killed in the Seminole War in 1835.

DADE COUNTY, 1841
Dadeville (Dade), 1841

Daviess, Col. Joseph Hamilton (1774-1811), who fell at Tippecanoe.

DAVIESS COUNTY, 1836

Gentry, Col. Richard, of Boone County, who fell in the Florida War.

GENTRY COUNTY, 1845

Pike, Gen. Zebulon Montgomery (1779-1813), explorer, who fell at Toronto.

PIKE COUNTY, 1818

Ramsay, Capt. Allen, who fell near Cap au Gris in battle with the Indians about 1815.

Ramsay Creek (Pike)

Ripley, Gen. Eleazer Wheelock (1782-1839), who was later a Congressman from Louisiana.

RIPLEY COUNTY, 1833

Sibley, Gen. George C. (1782-1863), Indian agent at Fort Osage 1818-1826.

Sibley (Jackson), 1844

Vernon, Col. Miles (1786-1866), who served in the Battle of New Orleans.

VERNON COUNTY, 1855

MEXICAN WAR (2)

Doniphan, Col. Alexander William (1808-1887), who led Missouri troops into Mexico.

Doniphan (county seat of Ripley), 1847

Worth, Gen. William Jenkins (1794-1849), second in command under General Taylor.

WORTH COUNTY, 1861

Here, of course, also belong Taylor, Fremont, and Stockton, who are listed elsewhere.

LATER WARS (3)

Bevier, Col. Robert; a noted Confederate leader.
Bevier (Macon), 1868

Chaffee, Gen. A. R. (1842-1914), of the Spanish-American War.
Chaffee (Scott), 1905

Pershing, Gen. John Joseph (1860-1948), who commanded American troops in World War 1.
Pershing (Gasconade), 1921
(changed from its earlier name of Potsdam)

NAVAL NAMES (15)

Decatur, Capt. Stephen (1779-1820), who won fame in the Tripolitan War.
Decatur (Cape Girardeau), 1803
Decatur (Cole), 1820
Decaturville (Camden), 1838
DECATUR COUNTY, 1843-1845
(name adopted for two years by Ozark Co.)

Dewey, Admiral George (1837-1917), who captured Manila in the Spanish-American War.
Dewey (Polk), 1898
Dewey School (St. Louis), 1917
(with other schools in Gentry, Wright and Jasper Cos.)

Farragut, Admiral David Glasgow (1801-1870), of Civil War fame.
Farragut School (St. Louis), 1905

Lawrence, Capt. James (1781-1813), who fell in the Chesapeake-Shannon fight.
LAWRENCE COUNTY (the first), 1815
LAWRENCE COUNTY (the second), 1843
Chesapeake (Lawrence), 1845

Perry, Capt. Oliver Hazard (1785-1819), who won the Battle of Lake Erie.
PERRY COUNTY, 1820
Perryville (county seat of Perry), 1822

Ringgold, Admiral Cadwalader, who charted the California coastline.
Ringgold (Platte), 1853

Stockton, Commodore Robert Field (1795-1866), who helped Fremont to conquer California.
Stockton (Cedar), 1857
(replacing the first name of Fremont)

Truxton, Capt. Thomas (1755-1822), who commanded privateers during the Revolutionary War.
Truxton (Lincoln), 1845

Our favorite naval name-fathers are obviously Decatur, Perry, and Lawrence, and this seems to be true in the rest of the country as well. We have used Lawrence as a county name twice, first in the burst of enthusiasm aroused by the news of his triumphant victory and death in 1813, for the abortive and over-large western county created in 1815, which almost immediately had to be broken up into more than a dozen new counties; and then in 1843 for the *Lawrence County* that still exists.

The number of these naval place-names in Missouri is truly astonishing, for such an inland State. According to a letter recently received from the Naval Academy at Annapolis, which is conducting a survey of its own of all the naval place names in the country, Missouri leads all the others States of the Union in paying tribute in this way to our heroes of the sea.

NAMES FROM STATE HISTORY (65)

While paying generous tribute in the selection of her place names to the leaders who have come to the nation from every other State in the Union, Missouri has by no means neglected her own sons. More than forty distinguished Missourians have been honored by having more than sixty places in the State named for them, including twenty-four of our counties.

GUBERNATORIAL PLACE NAMES (26)

We may take first our Governors, since the Louisiana Purchase of 1804. The earlier French and Spanish officials so honored have already been listed. More than half of our American Governors have left their names behind them on our map. They are here enumerated in chronological order.

a. Territorial

Captain Amos Stoddard (1762-1813), Acting Governor of Louisiana Territory, 1804-1805.
STODDARD COUNTY, 1835

Frederick Bates (1777-1825), Secretary of Louisiana Territory, 1806-1812; Secretary Missouri Territory, 1812-1821; Governor of the State of Missouri, 1824-1825.
BATES COUNTY, 1833

Meriwether Lewis (1774-1809), Explorer, Governor of Louisiana Territory, 1807-1809.
LEWIS COUNTY, 1833
Lewistown (Lewis), 1871

Benjamin Howard (1760-1814), Governor of Louisiana Territory, 1810-1813.

HOWARD COUNTY, 1816

William Clark (1770-1838), Explorer, Governor of Missouri Territory, 1813-1820.

CLARK COUNTY, 1836

b. State Governors (only the year of election or accession is given for each.)

1826: John Miller	**MILLER COUNTY,** 1837
1832: Daniel Dunklin	**DUNKLIN COUNTY,** 1845
1840: Thomas Reynolds	**REYNOLDS COUNTY,** 1845
1848: Austin A. King	**Kingston** (county seat of Caldwell), 1842
1857: Robert M. Stewart	**Stewartsville** (De Kalb), 1854
1864: Willard P. Hall	**Hall's Station** (Buchanan)
1864: Thomas C. Fletcher	**Fletcher** (Jefferson), 1896
1868: Joseph Washington	**McClurg** (Johnson), about 1868
McClurg	**McClurg** (Taney), 1872
1874: Charles Hardin	**Hardin** (Ray), 1868
1876: John S. Phelps	**PHELPS COUNTY,** 1857
1880: Thomas Theodore	
Crittenden	**Crittenden** (Camden), 1879
1884: John S. Marmaduke	**Marmaduke** (Dallas), 1869
	(now Redtop)
1887: A. P. Morehouse	**Morehouse** (New Madrid), 1893
1888: D. R. Francis	**Francis** (Audrain)
1900: Alexander M. Dockery	**Dockery** (Ray), 1889
1904: Joseph Wingate Folk	**Folk** (Osage)
	Wingate (Cass), 1904
1908: Herbert Spencer Hadley	**Hadley** (Reynolds), 1915
1929: Henry Stewart Caulfield	**Caulfield** (Howell), 1930

OTHER MISSOURI LEADERS (39)

Twenty-four other Missouri leaders, from all walks of life, have left a liberal allowance of place names behind them, including the names of 22 counties. Since it has proved difficult to get reliable dates for some of them, they are here listed in alphabetical order.

David R. Atchison (1807-1886), Senator, 1843-1855.

ATCHISON COUNTY, 1845

James H. Audrain: State Legislator from St. Charles, who died in office in 1831.

AUDRAIN COUNTY, 1836

David Barton (1783-1837), one of the first U. S. Senators from Missouri, elected in 1820, and served till 1830.

BARTON COUNTY, 1855

Thomas Hart Benton (1782-1858), Senator 1821-1851. Known as "Old Bullion."

> **Benton** (county seat of Scott), 1822
> **BENTON COUNTY,** 1835
> **Bullion's Landing** (Marion), 1844
> **Bullion** (Adair), 1872
> **Benton City** (Audrain), 1881
> **Bentonville** (Benton), 1891
> **Lake Benton,** 1931 (now usually
>   known as the Lake of the Ozarks)

Col. George Frederick Bollinger (1770-1842), who led German colonists into Missouri in 1800.

> **Fredericktown** (county seat of Madison), 1819
> **BOLLINGER COUNTY,** 1851

Daniel Boone (1735-1820). He came from Virginia to Kentucky in 1769, then from Kentucky to Missouri in 1799.

> **Boone's Lick Road or Trace,** 1807
> **Boonville** (Cooper), 1817
> **BOONE COUNTY,** 1820
> **Boone's Grave** (Warren), 1820
> **Boonsboro** (Howard), 1840

Zimri A. Carter, who came from South Carolina to Missouri in 1812.

> **CARTER COUNTY,** 1859

Sam Caruthers, who was Congressman from Southeast Missouri in 1852.

> **Caruthersville** (county seat of Pemiscot), 1857

Sarshall Cooper, who was killed by Indians near Arrow Rock in 1814.

> **COOPER COUNTY,** 1818

Lewis Dent, who came from Virginia to Missouri in 1835.

> **DENT COUNTY,** 1851

Albert G. Harrison (1800-1839) of Fulton, Congressman, 1835-1839.

> **Harrisonville** (county seat of Cass), 1837
> **HARRISON COUNTY,** 1845

Dr. David Rice Holt, who was a member of the State Legislature at the time of his death in 1840.

> **HOLT COUNTY,** 1841

Thomas Jefferson Howell, who came from Tennessee to Missouri in 1840; a member of the State Legislature.

> **HOWELL COUNTY,** 1857

James Lillard, member of the first State Legislature in 1820, but who later offended his constituents by writing an abusive letter.

> **LILLARD COUNTY,** 1820
>   (changed to Lafayette County in 1825)

Lewis F. Linn (1796-1843), Senator 1833-1843.
> **LINN COUNTY,** 1837
> **Linn** (county seat of Osage), 1838
> **Linneus** (county seat of Linn), 1840
> (at first called Linnville)

Spencer Darwin Pettis (1802-1831), a popular young Congressman who was killed in a famous duel with Major Thomas Biddle on the sandbar opposite St. Louis, on August 27, 1831.
> **PETTIS COUNTY,** 1833

Daniel Ralls, member of the State Legislature from Pike County, who died in office in 1820.
> **RALLS COUNTY,** 1820

John Ray, Member of the State Legislature in 1820.
> **RAY COUNTY,** 1820

Hiram Roberts, first settler in what is now Buchanan County, who came to Missouri before 1836.
> **ROBERTS COUNTY,** (so called before 1839,
> when it was changed to Buchanan County)

Major James Sidney Rollins (1812-1888). Editor and member of the State Legislature from Boone County, where he introduced on Jan. 24, 1839, an "Act to Select a Site for the State University." In 1872 he was officially awarded the title of "Father of the University."
> **ROLLINS COUNTY** (name proposed in 1856
> for a new county which never materialized)

John Scott (1782-1861). First Congressman from Missouri.
> **SCOTT COUNTY,** 1821

George F. Shannon (1785-1836). Served in the Lewis and Clark Expedition; later lived at St. Charles, where he was known as "Peg-Leg Shannon."
> **SHANNON COUNTY,** 1841
> **Peg-Leg Shannon Cemetery** (Marion), 1935

Gen. Thomas Adams Smith (1781-1844). Register of Public Lands at old Franklin in 1818, where he gave title to much of the land settled in the Boone's Lick Country. He was known as the "Cincinnatus of the West."
> **Smithton** (Boone), 1819 (first name of Columbia)

John W. Stone, an early settler, who came from Tennessee to Missouri.
> **STONE COUNTY,** 1851

The outstanding Missouri name-fathers are Boone, Linn, and Benton. There are at least a dozen lesser places besides those listed—creeks, townships, and schools—named for the rugged old pathfinder Daniel Boone in the

State. And there are more than thirty places named for him in other States, including seven other Boone Counties.

Nearly as many Missouri places bear the name of the popular Senator Linn, though it is not always easy to tell which of them was named for him and which for the "linn" or linden tree. The county seat originally called *Linnville* was clearly meant for him, but the Senator modestly suggested the substitution of the famous Swedish botanist's name—a rather transparent disguise.

The stormy career of Senator Thomas Hart Benton, the "Father of the West," as he was sometimes called, may be accurately charted in the places that were named for him. No fewer than twenty-five places big enough to appear on the map proudly bear his name today; and if all of the "little" names—the Benton schools, parks, streets, and the like—are added, the list would approach a hundred. Oldest is *Benton* in Scott County, named for him during his first year in the Senate. Ten years later a new county was named for him. In 1840, he had to fight one of his hardest battles, leading the wing of the party known as the "Hards" to victory over the "Softs," who stood for a liberal issue of paper money by the wildcat banks. It was in that campaign that he acquired his best known nickname, commemorated in *Bullion's Landing* at the mouth of the Fabius River in Marion County. In that year, however, he suffered his first defeat, when his name, which had been proposed for the county seat of Buchanan, was rejected in favor of *Sparta*. But "Old Bullion" still fought on.

Then in 1850 came the fierce political struggle that finally overthrew him. It was presaged when *Benton Township* in Texas County deliberately changed its name to *Cass Township;* for Lewis Cass, who had won the Democratic nomination for the Presidency in 1848, was one of his most formidable opponents. And yet, even after his defeat in 1851, and his death in 1858, he was still adored, perhaps for the very enemies he had made. The naming of *Benton Station* in suburban St. Louis in 1852, of *Benton Barracks* from 1860 to 1864, of *Benton City* in 1881, of *Bentonville* in 1891, and latest of all, by act of the State Legislature in 1931, of *Lake Benton* for the largest artificial body of water in the world (even though the forgetful public persists in calling it the *Lake of the Ozarks*), all are ample demonstration that "Old Bullion's" soul still goes marching on. There can be no doubt whatever that Benton is Missouri's favorite son.

C. PERSONAL NAMES (LOCAL) (309)

We now come to places named for what, somewhat arbitrarily, may be called local figures. The historical names listed in the previous section include many given for personages who may be considered to belong to national or State history. Those we shall now take up are of more limited and local importance. The line is not always easy to draw, of course. But taken as a whole, the local personal names do constitute a distinct and separate group.

The place names for local figures are always the most numerous of all. They are also at first sight the least interesting, except to their neighbors who knew them and remember them. But almost all of them were once men and women of enterprise and leadership, who played their parts in the building and progress of their local communities. Many of the places named for them have become among the largest and most important in the State. These names fall naturally into eight sub-groups.

POSTMASTERS AND OTHER PUBLIC OFFICIALS (28)

Whenever a place grew large enough to demand a post office, it fell to the first postmaster to send in an application to Washington, and with it his suggestion of a suitable name for the place. To satisfy the rules and regulations of the Postal Department, the name must not be the same or too similar to that of any post office previously established in the State; also it must be easy to read and write, and as short as possible. It was only human that postmasters should often yield to the temptation of sending in their own names, or those of members of their families or friends. Next to come to mind were naturally the names of prominent local officials.

Akers (Shannon), 1886 — John Akers, postmaster
Bahner (Pettis), 1886 — Edward Bahner, first postmaster
Branson (Taney), 1881 — R. S. Branson, first postmaster
Cameron (Clinton), 1855 — Judge Elisha Cameron
Campbell (Dunklin), 1886 — Judge Alexander Campbell
Covert (Texas), 1915 — J. A. Covert, postmaster
Cowgill (Caldwell), 1887 — Judge James Cowgill
Dameron (Lincoln), 1886 — Noah Dameron, postmaster
Easley (Boone) — W. G. Easley, postmaster
Holcomb (Dunklin), 1886 — Lewis Holcomb, county sheriff
Holden (Johnson), 1857 — Major W. B. Holden, member of the State Legislature
Kennett (county seat of Dunklin), 1867 — Luther Kennett, Mayor of St. Louis, and a great railroad promoter
King City (Gentry),1858 — King, Postmaster General in Washington at the time
Koeltztown (Osage), 1867 — August Koeltz, first postmaster
Lakenan (Shelby), 1876 — Robert Lakenan, member State Legislature

Lisle (Cass), 1892 — Judge J. D. Lisle
Lixville (Bollinger), 1897 — Louis W. Lix, first postmaster
Luebbering (Franklin), 1888 — John Frederick Luebbering, first postmaster

Mahan (Texas), 1904 — Mrs. Sam Mahan, postmistress
Oermann (Jefferson), 1889 — Charles Oermann, postmaster
Oyer (St. Clair)), 1886 — William Oyer, postmaster
Rea (Andrew), 1888 — Judge Joseph Rea
Reuter (Taney), 1880 — Reuter, first postmaster
Salisbury (Chariton), 1867 — Judge Lucien Salisbury, founder
Souden (Ozark), 1903 — G. W. Souden, first postmaster
Venable (Texas), 1892 — P. S. Venable, postmaster
Womack (Ste. Genevieve), 1895 — R. M. Womack, first postmaster
Wortham (St. Francois), 1925 — Ray Wortham, first postmaster

BUSINESS MEN: MILLERS, MERCHANTS, AND OTHERS (31)

Alley (Shannon), 1886 — John Alley, miller
Anthony's Mill (Washington), 1876 — Jonas M. Anthony, miller
Benoist (St. Francois), 1906 — Eugene H. Benoist, real estate
Bollard (Stoddard), 1889 — Bollard, sawmill operator
Bonnot's Mill (Osage), 1852 — Felix Bonnot, miller
Busick (Carter) — E. H. Busick, merchant
Caruth (Dunklin), 1881 — Caruth, merchant
Choat (Bollinger), 1899 — Albert Choat, storekeeper
Corkery (Dallas), 1895 — Mike Corkery, storekeeper
Crosno (Mississippi), 1891 — F. M. Crosno, merchant
Duenweg (Jasper) — Duenweg, promoter and merchant
Estes (Pike), 1887 — Estes, storekeeper
Farrar (Perry), 1893 — R. B. Farrar, merchant
Faucett (Buchanan), 1890 — Robert Faucett, miller
Gideon (New Madrid), 1900 — Frank Gideon, merchant
Gray Summit (Franklin), 1859 — Daniel Gray opened a famous old hotel here in 1845

Hough (New Madrid), 1910 — B. Hough, merchant
Huxie (Bollinger), 1901 — William J. Hux, sawmill operator
Kirksville (Adair), 1841 — Jesse Kirk, tavern keeper
Koester (St. Francois), 1895 — C. E. Koester, gristmill operator
Lemay (St. Louis) — Francois Le Mais, ferryman
Lowry City (St. Clair), 1871 — Lowry, merchant
Munger (Reynolds), 1867 — Marvin Munger, gristmill operator
Owensville (Gasconade), 1867 — Owen, storekeeper
Oxly (Ripley), 1885 — F. G. Oxley, business man of Cincinnati

Rively (Bates), 1888 — J. T. Rively, mining company
Skrainka (Madison), 1891 — Skrainka Construction Company
Sprott (Ste. Genevieve), 1904 — John Sprott, storekeeper
Steele (Pemiscot), 1897 — L. L. Steele, merchant

Stephens College in Columbia (Boone), so named in 1870 — James Leachman Stephens (1815-1902), merchant and philanthropist

Wellston (St. Louis), 1889 — Erastus Wells, who developed the streetcar system of St. Louis

It will be obvious that the millers of early days had a major part in starting new communities, as did merchant and storekeepers of all kinds. The keepers of taverns and hotels also had their part to play.

RAILROAD MEN (28)

The enormous part taken by the coming of the railroads to Missouri in the growth of the State is amply corroborated by nearly 30 place names that were borrowed from the names of railroad officials, operators, employees, and directors. Many of them had their own homes in distant localities. No attempt has been made in the following list to specify the particular road involved, for they were always changing, or the special function of the person who is commemorated, except to give his full name where it has been discovered.

Baring (Knox), 1889 — Baring Brothers of England, who made a large loan

Bagnell (Miller), 1882 — William Bagnell

Blodgett (Scott), 1869 — Wells H. Blodgett

Bolckow (Andrew), 1868

Durham (Lewis), 1876

Elayer (Crawford) — William Elayer, conductor

Eldon (Miller), 1881

Gower (Clinton), 1870 — A. G. Gower, Superintendent

Hunnewell (Shelby), 1857 — H. Hollis Hunnewell

Kearney (Clay), 1856 — Charles E. Kearney

Kirkwood (St. Louis), 1852 — James P. Kirkwood

La Due (Henry) 1870 — Judge A. D. Ladue

Maitland (Holt), 1880

Marquand (Madison), 1869 — W. G. Marquand

Melugin (Jasper), 1905

Moberly (Randolph), 1861 — Col. William E. Moberly, President of the road which is now part of the Wabash Railroad

Monett (Barry), 1887

Montier (Shannon), 1890 — A. N. Montier

Napier (Holt), 1882

Orrick (Ray), 1869 — W. W. Orrick

Pierce City (Lawrence), 1870 — Andrew Peirce of Boston, President of the Frisco Railroad

Rives (Dunklin), 1894 — Col. H. W. Rives, Superintendent

Saint Clair (Franklin), 1859 — Saint Clair, engineer

Seligman (Barry), 1880

Slater (Saline), 1889 — Col. John F. Slater of Chicago, director of the C. & A. R. R.

Sturgeon (Boone), 1856 — Isaas H. Sturgeon, Superintendent

Thayer (Oregon), 1886 — Nathaniel Thayer of Boston, an important stockholder

Thomure (Ste. Genevieve) — F. J. Thomure, Superintendent

PROFESSIONAL MEN (29)

This list of places that have adopted the names of well known and influential physicians, teachers, clergymen, and journalists reveals the vital part that has been taken in the upbuilding of Missouri by professional men of all varieties. If we had space to list all the local schools, colleges, and churches which are dedicated to the memory of beloved and respected teachers, preachers, and writers, their number would be greatly increased. That the instruction received in our schools, however, is not always as effective as could be wished is suggested by the fact that the former pupil of Miss Annet Lenox could not even remember how to spell her name correctly. Clergymen of all denominations are well represented on our map, as are newspaper men from papers in all parts of the State.

Anutt (Dent), 1891 — Miss Annet Lenox, teacher, by a former pupil who was a poor speller

Blewett High School (St. Louis), 1905 — Ben Blewett (1856-1917), Superintendent of Schools in St. Louis, 1908-1917

Bonfils (St. Louis), 1876 — Dr. Bonfils, who was a "beloved physician"

Chaminade (St. Louis), 1910 — The Venerable William Joseph Chaminade of Bordeaux, France, founder of the order of Brothers of St. Mary

Coleman, or Colman (St. Louis) — Col. Norman J. Colman (1827-1911), journalist, agriculturist, and Cabinet member. He was appointed in 1889 by President Cleveland our first Secretary of Agriculture

Demotte (Lafayette), 1881 — Mark L. Demotte, editor of the Lexington **Register**

Doss (Dent), 1889 — William Doss, printer, who worked on the Dent County **Democrat**

Ely (Marion), 1861, and West Ely (Marion), 1836 — Rev. Ezra Stiles Ely, founder of Marion College

Glennon (Bollinger), 1928, and Glennonville (Dunklin), 1904 — Archbishop John J. Glennon of St. Louis

Gorin (Scotland),1887 — Rev. M. G. Gorin (?)

Hagenbuck (Howell), 1936 — F. E. Hagenbuck, editor of the Kiowa **Record**

Harris Teachers College (St. Louis), 1905 — William Torrey Harris (1835-1909), Superintendent of Schools in St. Louis, 1867-1880, later U. S. Commissioner of Education

Hyde Park (St. Louis), 1854 — William Hyde (1836-1898), editor of the **Missouri Republican** in St. Louis, 1866-1885

Joplin (Jasper) 1873 — Rev. Harris G. Joplin, who established the first Methodist church in the county at his cabin in 1840

Lee's Summit (Jackson), 1865 — Dr. J. P. G. Lea (sic), who helped lay the town out

Marvin (Texas), 1901 — Bishop Enoch Mather Marvin, the "Grand Old Man of Missouri Methodism."

Mott (Howell), 1893 — Miss Martha Briscoe, teacher, known affectionally as "Aunt Mott"

Ramsey Creek (Cape Girardeau) — Andrew Ramsey (1746-1815) of Virginia, who settled here in 1795 and established the first English School west of the Mississippi River

Rosati (Phelps), 1930 — Bishop Joseph Rosati, second Catholic bishop of St. Louis

Sharpsburg (Marion), 1853 — Rev. Richard Sharp, an early circuit rider

Smith Academy (St. Louis), 1879 — Dr. James Smith, its founder

Soldan High School (St. Louis), 1909 — F. Louis Soldan (1842-1908), Superintendent of Schools in St. Louis, 1895-1908

Strother (Monroe), 1886 — Prof. Frank Strother of Strother Institute

Switzler Hall at Columbia, 1871 (oldest building on the State University campus, and **Switzler** (Audrain), 1870 — William Franklin Switzler (1819-1906), editor of the Columbia **Statesman** and historian

Tallent (Bollinger), 1902 — Rev. George W. Tallent

Treloar (Warren), 1899 — W. M. Treloar, Professor of Music at Hardin College

WOMAN'S PLACE IN MISSOURI NOMENCLATURE (75)

If any proof were needed that the women of Missouri are exceptionally fascinating, it would be supplied by the extraordinary propensity that Missourians have always had to name places for them. Hardly a county in the State but contains a handful of these charming names, although the Ozarks is perhaps the most gallant section. When one surveys the astonishing list of more than 75 women's names, scattered all over the State, it almost seems that the early Missourians made up their minds to use every feminine name in the book.

They have even preserved some quaint but delightful names that are seldom employed nowadays, such as *Iantha, Idalia, Izora, Meta, Neola,* and *Senath.* The familiar names are sometimes a little disguised, as in *Silva* for

Slyvia, *Vada* for Nevada, or *Mandeville* for Amanda, or in the pet-form "Sed" for Sarah. The fascination which this last name, in the expanded form of *Sedalia*, has had for towns in sister States all the way from the Atlantic to the Pacific, has been discussed in earlier pages.

Some places have even contrived to honor two ladies at the same time by combining their names, as *Annada* and *Ellenorah*. The postmaster at *Minimum* in Iron County meant to name that place for his wife Minnie, but he added a suffix that may have seemed to her just a trifle belittling. On the other hand, there was one adoring, or tactful, husband who actually canonized his wife, unofficially, by calling the town he laid out in Linn County *Saint Catherine*.

There are three feminine names of real historical interest. *Maryville* in Nodaway County was named in 1845 for the first white woman to live in the town. *Savanah* in Andrew County, founded in 1841, took the name of its first white child, who had been so christened by her parents in memory of their former home in Georgia. *Louisiana* in Pike County was named in 1818 for a little girl whose parents had brought her there from St. Louis only a short time before. She was fourteen years old in that year, and they had chosen that name for her because she was born in 1804, the year of the Louisiana Purchase.

Ada (Ray), 1854	Wife of Eli Carter, its founder
Agnes (Laclede), 1897	Wife of Charles Handley
Alice (Texas), 1888	Daughter of J. M. Embree, old settler
Alma (Lafayette), 1879	Daughter of John M. Woodson, founder
Amanda (Crawford), before 1857	Wife of George M. Jamison, postmaster
Annada (Pike), 1886	Ann and Ada, daughters of Carson Jamison, an old settler
Annapolis (Iron), 1876	Anna, wife of Thomas Allen, R.R. president, with a side glance at Annapolis, Maryland
Augusta (St. Charles), 1836	Wife of Leonard Harrold, its founder
Bernie (Stoddard), 1890	Bernice, daughter of George S. Crumb, its founder
Berthaville (Randolph), 1886	Bertha lived in the town
Catherine (St. Clair), 1891	Daughter of the postmaster
Chloe (St. Clair), 1900	Daughter of Dr. Phillips, a physician there
Clara (Texas), 1902	Wife of Haden Lynch, postmaster
Cornelia (Johnson), 1853	Wife of Dr. Love, who lived there
Dixie (Callaway), 1892	Daughter of S. H. Powell, postmaster
Ellendale (St. Louis)	Ellen, daughter of William L. Thomas, publisher and author

Ellenorah (Gentry) — Ellen and Norah, daughters of a resident

Elizabeth (first county seat of Callaway), before 1826 — Wife of Henry Brite, pioneer settler

Emma (Lafayette), 1895 — Daughter of Rev. H. C. Bemetrio, Lutheran minister at Concordia

Enid (Morgan), 1899 — Wife of founder

Esther (St. Francois), 1901 — Daughter of Harry Cantwell, business man

Ethlyn (Lincoln), 1910 — Daughter of George Brown, who lived there

Eudora (Polk) — Unidentified

Eugenia (Crawford) — Daughter of Ferguson, a landowner

Geraldine (Wright), 1893 — Daughter of the postmaster

Helena (Andrew), 1878 — Daughter of a railroad official

Hester (Marion), 1848 — Unidentified

Iantha (Barton), 1881 — Unidentified

Idalia (Stoddard), 1890 — Daughter of H. H. Bedford, landowner (?)

Irena (Worth), 1876 — Wife of William Richard, early settler

Izora (Chariton), 1851 — Wife of Edward Irvine, miller

Juanita (New Madrid), 1902 — Daughter of Greer, miller

Laura (Scotland), 1860 — Unidentified

Louisa (Texas), 1910 — Wife of Jim Embree, postmaster

Louisiana (Pike), 1818 — Louisiana Basye, afterwards Mrs. L. Tombs, was born in St. Louis in 1804. Her father John Walter Basye gave her that name because the Louisiana Purchase came in the year of her birth.

Lucia (Taney), 1902 — Wife of E. P. Brice, postmaster

Lulu (Dunklin), 1883 — By Judge E. J. Langdon, for "one of my old sweethearts"

Manda (Gasconade), 1899 — Daughter of the postmaster

Mandeville (Carroll), 1854 — Miss Amanda Shirley, who lived there

Marceline (Linn), 1887 — Wife of a railroad official

Margaret (Gasconade), 1896 — Unidentified

Marthasville (Warren), 1818 — Wife of Dr. John Young, founder (?)

Mary Institute (St. Louis), 1859 — Daughter of Dr. James Smith, founder

Maryville (county seat of Nodaway), 1845 — Mrs. Mary Graham, first white woman in the town

Maud (Shelby), 1886 — Daughter of Ridings, first postmaster

Maurine (Henry), 1885 — Daughter of W. H. Dorman, who lived there

Meta (Osage), 1904 — Sister of Schreifer, local landowner

Mildred (Taney), 1906 — Daughter of first postmaster

Minimum (Iron), 1910 — Minnie, wife of Dr. N. A. Farr, postmaster

Naomi (Marion), 1876 — Unidentified

Neola (Dade), 1889 — Unidentified

Octavia (Scotland) — Unidentified

Olga (Douglas), 1910 — Wife or daughter of first postmaster

Opal (Lawrence) — Unidentified

Pansy (Douglas), 1899 — Daughter of postmaster

Regina (Jefferson), 1886 — Sister of Isador Mandle, resident

Roselle (Madison), 1896 — A showgirl who pleased the town (?); or perhaps for Rose and Ella, daughters of an old settler (?)

Ruby (New Madrid) — Miss Ruby Reeves, who lived there

Ruth (Texas), 1876 — Wife of J. M. Embree (Cf. Alice)

Saint Catherine (Linn), 1856 — Mrs. Catherine Elliott, by her husband, William Elliott

Savannah (Andrew), 1841 — Savannah Woods, first white child born in the town, named by her parents for their old home in Savannah, Georgia

Sedalia (Pettis), 1857 — Sarah Elvira Smith (known as "Sed"), by her father, Gen. George R. Smith, founder of the town

Senath (Dunklin), 1882 — Senath Hale Douglass, by her husband, A. W. Douglass, founder of the town

Silva (Wayne), 1909 — Sylvia (pronounced locally "Silva"), a friend of the postmistress

Stella (Newton), 1870 — Unidentified

Sue City (Macon), 1868 — Wife of Joseph T. Ryster, local landowner

Susanna (Webster), 1893 — Wife of Jim Cunningham, local landowner

Teresita (Shannon), 1904 — Unidentified

Theodosia (Ozark)), 1887 — Wife of J. M. Herd, first postmaster

Tina (Carroll), 1892 — Daughter of E. M. Gilchrist, railroad man

Una (Jackson) — Wife of a railroad official

Vada (Texas), 1918 — Nevada Jackson, daughter of the postmaster

Vera (Pike), 1904 — Daughter of J. C. Spears, hotel keeper.

Viola (Barry), 1894 — Unidentified

Virginia Mines (Franklin), 1832 — Daughter of Bundrage, mine owner

MASCULINE FIRST AND MIDDLE NAMES (26)

The genial Missouri custom of using the first or Christian name of a friend or of anyone particularly liked or admired is abundantly exemplified among Missouri place names. Masculine names, naturally, are not quite so attractive as names for places as are feminine names. But an outstanding case is the name of *Andrew County,* whether or not it was given in honor of a local political leader, one Andrew Jackson Davis, or as I think more likely for the idolized President Andrew Jackson himself.

A lively controversy was waged in the newspapers of Madison County a few years ago over the origin of the name of its county seat, *Fredericktown.* Older historians have all maintained that it was named for George Frederick Bollinger, the sturdy pioneer who led the first large band of German-American settlers across the Mississippi in 1800, and for whom, nine years after his death, the present county of Bollinger was named in 1851. When *Fredericktown* was founded in 1819, Colonel Bollinger was a prominent member of the General Assembly of the Territoy; and his name is said to have been proposed by his friend and fellow member Nathaniel Cook, to whom belonged the land on which the new village was laid out. I have accordingly listed it among names given above that were conferred for outstanding Missouri leaders.

This explanation has, however, been vigorously challenged, on the ground that it is hard to believe in any such use of a man's midde name, which is seldom well known even to his admirers. Why, it is asked, was the place not called Bollinger, or Georgetown? The answer to those questions is that perhaps Bollinger was felt as a bit difficult to pronounce, as it still is to many outsiders; and Georgetown would surely have been taken as meant for a still greater hero, George Washington, as it was in the case of *Georgetown* in Pettis County.

The rival theory has been put forward that *Fredericktown* was named for Frederick Bates, who was at that time Secretary of the Territory, and for whom *Bates County* was named in 1833. Alternately, it was suggested that it might have been named for Frederick the Great, presumably a hero in the eyes of the incoming German immigrants. No positive evidence, however, has been produced for either supposition.

It is perfectly true that most Americans today make little use of their middle names. Many reduce them to mere initials; and oddly enough, in a surprising number of cases that middle initial is only a letter and stands for nothing. The most conspicuous example is the name of President Harry S. Truman. I believe he has never revealed just what the letter S. in his name stands for, if anything.

So characteristic of Americans has become this lonely middle initial that the London magazine *Punch* made a jest of it a few years ago. This was a typical skit entitled "Sherlock Holmes Disguises Himself as an American." The great detective was about to venture across the Atlantic on one of his relentless manhunts. With his accustomed thoroughness, he neglected no detail of dress, accent, or personal habits that might help him to pass himself off as an unmistakable Yankee. As a final touch of perfection, he even had a new set of visiting cards engraved, reading "Sherlock P Holmes" —taking pains to omit the period, for it was just a P and nothing more!

There are still some Americans, however, who prefer to write out their middle names in full and use them freely. There must have been more in Missouri in early days, for quite a number of other towns are known to have adopted middle names. We have already listed among names for Presidents and Governors the towns of *Quincy* for John Quincy Adams, *Woodrow* for Thomas Woodrow Wilson, and *Wingate* for Joseph Wingate Folk. In the following list of local citizens we find the same phenomenon in the names of *Dillard, Racola, Madisonville,* and *Vilander.*

Aaron (Bates), 1892.
Aaron Stayton, who lived there.

Abesville (Stone), 1883.
Abe Payne, landowner.

Adelbert (Washington), 1924.
Adelbert E. Stockings, merchant.

Adrian (Bates), 1880
Son of Talmage (see below)

Alba (Jasper), 1882.
First name of the first postmaster.

ANDREW COUNTY, 1841
?Andrew Jackson Davis, local lawyer (according to the county history). Or for President Andrew Jackson?

Archie (Cass), 1880.
Son of Talmage (see below)

Arthur (Vernon), 1881.
Son of Talmage (see below)

Buell (Montgomery), 1903.
Buell Hensley, business man.

Cato (Barry), 1894.
Cato, an old Indian who lived there.

Clarence (Shelby), 1858.
Son of John Duff, railroad contractor.

Deventer (Mississippi), 1910.
Deventer Miller, business man.

Dillard (Crawford), 1887.
Joseph Dillard Cottrell, operator of a grist mill.

Festus (Jefferson), 1886.
Unidentified. (See below)

Lilbourn (New Madrid), 1903.
Lilbourn Lewis, landowner.

Madisonville (Ralls), 1836.
James Madison Crossthwaite, resident. (In 1856 another Madisonville in Mercer County was planned to honor President Madison, but had to be changed to Modena)

Milo (Vernon), 1881.
Milo Main, old resident.

Norborne (Carroll), 1868.
Norborne B. Coats, promotor of the town.

Ocie (Ozark), 1907.
Ocie Conklin, resident.

Orla (Laclede), 1886.
Son of a miller who lived there.

Racola (Washington), 1899.
John Racola Coleman, landowner.

Rhyse (Dent), 1921.
Rhyse Jeffries, son of a prominent landowner.

Rolla (county seat of Phelps), 1858.
Unidentified. (See below)

Sheldon (Vernon), 1881.
Son of Talmage (see below)

Vilander (Crawford), 1886.   Calvin Vilander Lynch, whose wife was the first postmistress.

Zalma (Bollinger), 1891.   Zalma Block, a friend of Louis Houck, the railroad builder.

The influential Mr. Talmage, who was General Passenger Agent for the Missouri Pacific Railroad, succeeded in having stations named for each of his four sons *Adrian, Archie, Arthur,* and *Sheldon.*

One of the most puzzling problems of Missouri nomenclature is the true origin of the name of *Rolla,* the county seat of Phelps. Usually when we are compelled to leave unsolved the source of a place name, the reason is sheer lack of information, the records having been lost. In the case of *Rolla,* however, we have too many explanations rather than too few. At least three conflicting stories, none of them too well supported, have been told about its origin. Two of them must be fictitious; perhaps all three are merely products of our Missouri genius for inventing good stories when reliable facts are unavailable.

The story most widely repeated has it that when the town was laid out in 1858, the citizens, most of whom were North Carolinians, wanted to name it for the capital city of the Tar Heel State. Being no great scholars, however, none of them could remember exactly how the name of their home town was spelled. They did the best they could, and the result was *Rolla;* i.e., Raleigh as they then pronounced it. This tale harmonizes beautifully with our Midwestern habits of speech; for if Missouri in our mouths turns regularly into "Mizzoura," why should not Raleigh become *Rolla?* And yet, perhaps, this story is just too good a one to be true. Experience teaches us that the better a story is, as a story, the less likely it is to be authentic. Dull facts are usually more like real life than clever fiction.

Another explanation that has been given is naturally disliked in *Rolla* itself. According to this version, the town was named for a dog. It seems there was disagreement among the early settlers over the exact location of their new town. The winning faction tried to appease the disgruntled minority by offering to let them choose the name. But the losers refused to be placated. In disgust they decided to name it for one of the mangiest of the many "houn' dawgs" that roamed the Ozark countryside. The hound's name happened to be Rollo; but they changed it to *Rolla* because towns are usually feminine. Now it is known that several other Missouri communities have acquired canine names, and Rollo is plausible enough for such a name. But the anecdote is a little too ingenious to be entirely credible.

The third account affirms that the place was really named for a character in a play. Sheridan's "Pizarro," a translation from the German dramatist Kotzebue, was just then immensely popular and was being performed throughout the country. In 1832, for instance, it was selected for the very first dramatic performance ever given in the drama-loving town of Columbia, Missouri. The sub-title of this old melodrama is "The Death of Rolla," for the leading role in it is sustained by a swashbuckling hero named Rolla, who was greatly admired by Missouri audiences. So the citizens of the prospective Phelps County town decided to name their adventurous community for him.

This last explanation is, I think, the one to be preferred, for the simple season that it could hardly have been invented afterwards, seeing that the current stage success was soon completely forgotten. But there is one slight modification in it that could be made, to increase its likelihood. We know the old hero had many namesakes among Missourians, who have always liked to give their children high-sounding and adventurous names. One of them, for example, was the eminent Rolla Wells (1856-1944), Mayor of St. Louis from 1901-1905. He was too young in 1858 to be the name-father of the town of *Rolla;* but there were doubtless a sufficiency of other Rollas in the 50s who were admired in Phelps County. Similar may be the true origin of another puzzlng name, *Festus,* about which much unsupported guesswork has been indulged. Festus has always been a rather common first name among Americans, particularly those of Irish descent, as for example the well-known Festus J. Wade (1859-1927), the St. Louis banker. He or some older Festus is much more likely to have inspired that name than the Festus of the Bible, who was a rather unsavory character, or the once popular but now forgotten poem entitled "Festus" by the English writer Bailey. We can only hope that some day authentic records will turn up to settle both of these intriguing mysteries.

FAMILY NAMES (20)

Many places were named not for any one individual, but for some highly respected family living in the neighborhood. Some of them, of course, may have had in mind a particular member of the family who has not as yet been identified. The twenty listed here in this category could easily be multiplied many times over.

Banister (Camden), 1895.

Barnumton (Camden), 1868. For the Barnum family.

Ben Avis (St. Louis), For the Avis family, with "Ben" prefixed on the Scotch model of Ben Lomond, etc.

Biehle (Perry), 1876.

Boekerton (New Madrid), 1910. For the Boeker family.

Casto (Shannon), 1897. For the Casto family (?).

Chitwood (Jasper).

Dagonia (Reynolds), 1907.

Dozier (St.Louis).

Fortescue (Holt). The family originally spelled it Fortesque.

Guber (Reynolds), 1912.
Huiscamp (Marion), 1890.
Kruegerville (Warren), 1885. For the Krueger family.
Laquey (Pulaski), 1900.
Latour (Johnson), 1885.
Loehr (St. Louis), 1899.
Noel (McDonald), 1887.
Ruble (Reynolds), 1899.
Saverton (Ralls), 1819.
Sudheimer (Maries), 1910.

LANDOWNERS AND PIONEERS (72)

We come now to the last and longest sub-group in this section, the farmers, founders, and homesteaders.

Algire (Washington), 1910. A farmer who lived near by.
Ancell (Scott), 1915. Pashal Ancell, early settler.
Argentville (Lincoln), 1886. Raleigh Argent, early settler.
Arnold (New Madrid), 1915. J. L. Arnold, landowner.
Aud (Osage), 1890. Joseph Aud, landowner.
Aullville (Lafayette), 1822. John and Robert Aull, pioneers.
Ayres (Saline), 1882. B. F. Ayres, farmer.
Bowdry Lake (Carroll), 1885. Ben Bowdry, landowner.
Brashear (Adair), 1872. Richard Brashear, who laid it out.
Brentwood (St. Louis). Brent laid out the town.
Brevator (Lincoln), 1880. John Brevator, landowner.
Bronaugh (Vernon), 1886. W. C. Bronaugh, landowner.
Brookfield (Linn), 1859. John Woods Brooks surveyed it.
Bunceton (Cooper), 1868. Harvey Bunceton laid it out.
Carlisle (Texas), 1867. R. W. Carlisle, landowner.
Carl Junction (Jasper). Charles Carl laid it out.
Cashion (Perry), 1901. A. H. Cashion, landowner.
Catron (New Madrid), 1895. W. C. Catron, early settler.
Clayton (county seat of St. Louis), 1877. Ralph Clayton, landowner.
Creighton (Cass), 1855. John B. Creighton, early settler.
Davault Creek (Bollinger). James Davault, pioneer, who came from North Carolina in 1804.
Davis (Dade). J. W. Davis, landowner.
Debery (Laclede). John Debery, landowner.
Diehlstadt (Scott), 1868. Col. H. J. Diehl (or Deal), German settler.
Dumas (Clark), 1889. A farmer who lived near by.
Elsberry (Lincoln), 1879. Robert T. Elsberry, landowner.
Elvins (St. Francois), 1892. Jesse M. Elvins, landowner.
Faust (Pemiscot), 1914. Two landowners, Faust or Foust.
Ferguson (St. Louis), 1876. William B. Ferguson, early settler, who came in 1845.

Foristell (St. Charles), 1856 (?) — Pierre Foristell, prominent citizen.
Glasgow (Howard), 1836. — James Glasgow, early settler.
Hahn (Bollinger), 1895. — J. W. G. Hahn, early settler.
Hart (McDonald), 1883. — W. B. Hart lived near by.
Hartville (county seat of Wright) — Isaac Hart, early settler.

Harviell (Butler), 1873. — Simeon Harviell, landowner.
Heagy (Stoddard), 1920. — Louis Heagy, landowner.
Higginsville (Lafayette), 1869. — Harvey J. Higgins, landowner.
Houck (Cape Girardeau), 1889. — Peter and Abraham Houk, landowners.

Huntsville (county seat of Randolph), 1829. — Daniel Hunt, early settler.
Jacksonville (Randolph), 1866. — Hancock Jackson, early settler.
Jadwin (Dent), 1879. — J. A. Jadwin lived near by.
Jaudon (Cass), 1893. — James A. Jaudon, landowner.
Keytesville (Chariton), 1832. — James Keyte, early settler.
Knoche (Jackson), bef. 1935. — Joseph Knoche, landowner.
Laddonia (Audrain), 1871. — Amos Ladd helped lay it out.
La Monte (Pettis), 1870. — A friend of the postmaster's.
Lathrop (Clinton), 1867. — An early settler.
Levasy (Jackson). — William Livesay (sic), landowner.
McCredie (Callaway), 1871. — George P. McCredie laid it out.
Machens (St. Charles), 1897. — Andrew Machen lived near by.
Mashek (Lincoln), 1889. — John Mashek lived near by.
Novinger (Adair), 1878. — John C. Novinger laid it out.
Owen (Lincoln), 1884. — James W. Owen, landowner.
Quarles (Henry), 1887. — Benjamin L. Quarles, landowner.
Ramsey's Creek (St. Charles), after 1800.
Ramsey's Bluff (Boone). — Capt. William Ramsey (1741-1845), a soldier in the Revolutionary War, who settled in St. Charles Co. in 1800. He died in Boone County at the age of 104.

Rowena (Audrain), 1884. — Hiley Rowe laid it out.
Sherrill (Texas), 1874. — John and Joel Sherrill, landowners.
Sikeston (Scott), 1860. — John Sikes laid it out.
Stahl (Adair), 1882. — S. F. Stahl laid it out.
Stanberry (Gentry), 1880. — John J. Stanberry, landowner.
Steelville (county seat of Crawford), 1836. — James Steel, landowner.
Sullivan (Franklin), 1860. — Stephen Sullivan, landowner.
Teagues (Webster), 1880. — An early settler.
Tipton (Moniteau), 1858. — William Tipton Seely laid it out.
Troutt (Washington), 1891. — William Troutt, landowner.
Ulman (Miller), 1896 — A landowner.
Vanduser (Scott), 1895. — John Vanduser, landowner.
Virgin Creek (Bollinger). — Virgin ('hard g'), landowner.
Warrensburg (county seat of Johnson), 1836. — Martin Warren, pioneer.
Webb City (Jasper), 1873. — John C. Webb laid out the town.
Zwanzig (Morgan), 1895. — Augustus Zwanzig, landowner.

Such a dry list of merely local figures, little known outside their own homes, who lived their quiet lives and died without fanfare or publicity, may seem at first commonplace and uninteresting. But when we remember how much these men, pioneers or sons of the pioneers, settlers and homesteaders and landowners, who plowed the fields and built the highways and laid out the towns and villages of Missouri, have really contributed to the making of our State, we come to realize that the names they have left behind them really have the greatest human interest of all. Doubtless many of them deserved the same moving tribute that was paid by our gifted poet Nicholas Vachel Lindsay to his "Proud Farmer of Indiana":

> Into the acres of the new-born State
> He poured his strength and plowed his ancient name.
> His plowmen neighbors were as lords to him.
> He lived a democrat, well nigh a king.
> For forty years he preached and plowed and wrought;
> And, for his lifetime, saved the countryside!

At any rate, these local citizens and plain people have earned one of the most lasting of all forms of immortality, a place on the map!

D. TOPOGRAPHICAL NAMES (191)

The topographical names are the ones that tie us closest to geography. They are very old and extremely numerous. There are perhaps as many of them as there are of either the historical or the personal names listed in the two previous sections. Indeed, it has been asserted, somewhat doubtfully, that all place names conferred by primitive peoples, the Indians, early English, Teutons, and Slavs, were topographical or descriptive in character. But such names are better suited to the natural features of a country, its creeks and rivers, lakes and mountains, than to artificial and man-made places like towns and cities—though they do include the names of eight of our Missouri counties. Hence we shall list fewer than two hundred of them here, attempting merely to give examples of all their principal varieties and sub-varieties. They include names that are definitive of location, descriptive of landscape, and informative of soil and mineral wealth, names of flora and of fauna, and finally names expressing approbation or disapprobation. Most of them are self-explanatory.

NAMES OF LOCATION (23)

These defining names do not show much imagination, but are always convenient. They give direction, north, east, south, and west, with relation to other places, or centrality of position. Missourians are especially fond of such terms as central or middle, which is to be expected of our central State. It has been said that *Centralia*, which was deliberately invented when the Boone County town was laid out in 1857, has the most ingenious and appropriate name in the entire State. Indeed, it might have been a happier name for the State itself, in which East and West, North and South, have always met and mingled as nowhere else in the Union, than is our accidental and historically inappropriate name of Missouri. Here are 23 of these names of location, which might easily be multiplied to more than a hundred.

Centertown (Cole), 1867
Centerview (Johnson), 1869
Centerville (county seat of Reynolds), 1847
Central College (Howard), 1855
Centralia (Boone), 1857
East Prairie (Mississippi)
Middletown (Montgomery), 1834
Midway (Cooper), 1833
Northern Heights (Clay)
North Kansas City (Clay)
North River (Knox, Shelby, Marion)
Norwood (Wright), 1882
Pemiscot Bayou ("running beside")
PEMISCOT COUNTY, 1851
Piedmont (Wayne), 1871

South River (Marion, etc.)
Southeast Missouri State College (Cape Girardeau), 1873
Southwest City (McDonald), 1870
Topozark (Washington), 1910
TWO RIVERS COUNTRY (Marion), before 1822
  (for territory between North and South Rivers)
Westboro (Atchison), ab. 1885
West Plains (county seat of Howell), 1850
Westport (Jackson), 1833

DESCRIPTIVE NAMES (44)

These are more varied, and tell us of size and age, altitude and situation. They mention distinctive local features, show some feeling for the incomparable beauty of our landscapes, and often add a touch of color. The region around Kansas City was aptly called the "Blue Country" in early days, before they regrettably thought fit to change its name to Jackson County. Our famous Missouri mud is conspicuously advertised in more than 50 of our place names, including 3 Muddy Branches, 4 Muddy Forks, 7 Muddy Creeks, and 9 Mud Creeks, to say nothing of our 6 Greasy Creeks, the French names using "bourbeuse," "marais," or "vase," and the original Osage name for our largest river, the *Ni-shodse*.

Altamont (Daviess), 1890
Auxvasse (Callaway), 1873 ("vases," marshes)
Bayouville (New Madrid), 1882
Big Blue River (Jackson)
Big Spring (Carter)
Blackwater (Cooper), 1887
Blackwater Creek (Pettis)
BLUE COUNTRY (Jackson), before 1826
Blue Spring (Wayne)
Bourbeuse River (Franklin) (i.e., "muddy")
Bristleridge (Johnson)
Chamois (Osage), 1856 (for its Alpine scenery)
Deepwater (Henry), 1885
Eminence (county seat of Shannon), 1870
  (for Old Eminence, which really was on a hill)
Flat River (St. Francois)
Glendale (St. Louis)
Grand River (i.e., "big")
Greasy Creek (Cass, Barry, Dallas, Madison, Ste. Genevieve, Wayne)
  ("greasy" in Missouri dialect means merely "muddy")
Greenfield (county seat of Dade), 1841
Greenville (county seat of Wayne), 1819
Hillsboro (county seat of Jefferson), 1839
Knob Lick (St. Francois), 1876
Little Blue River (Jackson)
Little River (New Madrid, etc.)
Marais Croche (St. Charles) ("crooked marsh or lake")

MARIES COUNTY, 1855 (for Marais)
Mountain Grove (Wright), 1878
Muddy (Caldwell), 1876
Newburg (Phelps), 1883
New Franklin (Howard), 1828
New London (county seat of Ralls), 1819
Nuevo Madrid, 1788
Ni-shodse (the "Muddy River")
Old Boone Home (St. Charles), 1810
Old Mines (Washington), 1830
Platte River (i.e., "flat, shallow")
PLATTE COUNTY, 1828
Redtop (Dallas) 1889
SALINE COUNTY, 1820 (i.e., "salt springs")
Salt River (Monroe, Ralls, Pike)
University City (St. Louis), 1906
Valley Park (St. Louis), 1887
White River
Whitewater River

NAMES OF SOIL AND MINERAL WEALTH (25)

Missouri place names alone would establish beyond question the inexhaustible riches of our soil and our mineral wealth, especially in lead and iron.

Acid (Franklin) (used in the iron mines)
Baryties (Washington), 1895 (barium sulphate)
Crystal City (Jefferson), 1868 (glassware)
Cuivre River (Lincoln) (where copper is not found)
Gravois Creek (Franklin) (i.e., "gravel")
Galena (county seat of Stone), 1853 (lead ore)
Golden City (Barton) (some gold was found here)
Graniteville (Iron), 1876
Hematite (Jefferson), 1861 (iron ore)
IRON COUNTY, 1857
Irondale (Washington), 1867
Iron Mountain (St. Francois), 1836
Ironton (county seat of Iron), 1853
Kaolin (Iron) (pottery clay)
Leadanna (Iron) (on the model of Susanna, Marianna, etc.)
Leadwood (St. Francois), 1910
Marble Hill (county seat of Bollinger), 1868
Mineral Point (Washington), 1867
Rich Hill (Bates), 1880
Rocheport (Boone), 1825
Rock Bridge (Boone)
Rockport (county seat of Atchison), 1851
Silex (Lincoln), 1886 (silica)
Syenite (St. Francois), 1881 (feldspar)
Wheatland (Hickory), 1869

NAMES OF FLORA AND FORESTRY (48)

Whatever may be true about the tree that once grew in Brooklyn, there are also many fine trees in Missouri, although the State is no longer the woodland paradise it once was when the white man arrived. Unimpeachable evidence of the incredible profusion and singular beauty of our primeval Missouri forests survives in our place names. We have in Missouri more than 1200 tree names.

We can even reconstruct, from place-name evidence alone, much of the character and distribution of those rich woodland resources that have been so tragically wasted. A fascinating map might be drawn of the tree names in the State, which would clearly distinguish a pine and cypress region in the south, a cedar, hickory, and linden section mainly in the west, and an oak division in the north and east. The beech tree is of course not a native of Missouri at all, except in its southeast corner; and our handful of beech names is correspondingly confined to the "bootheel."

Among our forest names, the sturdy oak leads all the rest, with nearly 400 name-children: 120 Oak Groves, 40 Oak Ridges, and as many Oakdales, Oaklands, and Oak Hills, not to mention all the Black Oaks and Black Jacks, Chestnut Oaks, Iron Oaks, Live Oaks, Pin Oaks, Post Oaks, Red Oaks, and White Oaks. Next in number are the 150 cedar names, including *Cedar County,* and 130 hickory names, although *Hickory County* can hardly in fairness be listed among them, for it was named for tough old Andrew Jackson, who was known as "Old Hickory."

There are over 100 pine-tree names, including the "pineries" and all the "piney" places: groves, creeks, bluffs, hills, and hollows. The elm and walnut names number nearly 100 each. There are about 50 names for the maple, 40 for the willow, and 30 each for the locust and the linden—the last-named being generally abbreviated in Missouri to "linn." It has, however, no right to *Linn County,* which was named for Senator Lewis F. Linn; but it can claim *Lindenwood College* and several *Linwoods.*

Not quite so numerous as these ten leading denizens of our forests, but still well represented, are names taken from the cottonwood, cypress, sycamore, gum, ash, dogwood, and hackberry. There are only five or six names for the poplar (including *Poplar Bluff*), the birch, the persimmon, and the pawpaw, and three or four for alder, holly, and catalpa. The exotic magnolia quite naturally has but two or three namesakes. It is more surprising that the familiar chinquapin has provided only three names, all being down in McDonald County.

The late Mr. W. N. Barron of Poplar Bluff, one of Missouri's greatest lumbermen and town builders, had an original idea once for breaking the monotony of our omnipresent tree names. A very interesting letter from him in our files tells how he used the botanical equivalents instead, in coining names for several towns he helped to found: *Celtis, Fagus, Ilex, Nyssa, Platanus, Quercus,* and *Ulmus.* Speaking of *Fagus,* he writes of his astonishment at actually finding a few beech trees in Butler County, whereupon he chose the Latin word for beech as the name for his future city.

Alder Hollow (Ste. Genevieve)
Ash Grove (Greene), 1853
Bendavis (Texas), 1910   (for the well-known apple)
Birch Tree (Shannon), 1865
Bois d'Arc (Greene), 1878 (the "Osage orange" or bow-wood)
Catalpa (Mississippi), 1880
Catawba (Caldwell), 1884
Cedar City (Callaway), 1870
CEDAR COUNTY, 1845
Celtis (Butler)   (the hackberry)
Chinquapin Hollow (McDonald)
Cottonwood Point (Pemiscot), 1867
Cypress (Harrison), 1892
Decypri (New Madrid), 1823
Dogwood (Douglas), 1903
Elm Point (St. Charles), 1890
Fagus (Butler), 1910   (the beech)
Gum Creek (Miller)   (gum trees)
Hackberry Creek (Vernon)
Hazelville (Knox), 1886
Hickory (Grundy)
Hollywood (Dunklin), 1900
Ilex (Butler)   (the holly)
Linden (first county seat of Atchison), 1848
Lindenwood College (St. Charles), 1827
Linn Creek (once county seat of Camden), 1841
Locust Grove (Henry), 1857
Magnolia (Johnson), 1896
Maplewood (St. Louis), 1893
Nyssa (Butler), 1910   (the tupelo or sweet gum)
Oakwood (Marion), 1888
Paw Paw (New Madrid), 1888
Persimmon Creek (Taney)
Pine Lawn (St. Louis), 1904
The Pinery (St. Francois)
          (Missouri dialect for a grove of pine trees)
Pineville (McDonald), 1847
Piney Spring (Phelps)
Platanus (Butler),   (the sycamore)
Poplar Bluff (Butler), 1850
Quercus (Butler), 1906   (the oak)
Slabtown Valley (Wayne), 1866,   (a busy saw-mill camp
Sugar Creek (Clark),   (for the sugar maples)
Sycamore (Ozark), 1891
Sylvania (Dade), 1865
Ulmus (Butler)   (the elm)

Viburnum (Crawford), 1904   (the honeysuckle)
Walnut Grove (Greene)
Willow Springs (Howell), 1868

NAMES OF FAUNA (25)

Missouri was once a paradise for hunters. If the Missouri Conservation Commission, which is doing so much to restore our earlier wealth in wild life, desires proof of this statement, it need use only the testimony supplied by our place names. More than 500 localities within our State derive their names from eight of the larger game animals alone, nearly all of which must have been originally conferred because these animals abounded in their vicinity. Yet today in many a spot so named not a single specimen of the beast whose name it bears has been seen within the memory of man. Only the names are left us, silent and melancholy witnesses of appalling waste of natural resources.

There are over a hundred places named for deer and elk, buck and doe: 20 Deer Creeks, Ridges, Runs, Parks, Fields, and Licks; 35 Elk Forks, Groves, Hollows, Rivers, and Sloughs, with 40 or more named for the buck and 10 for the does. The three noblest of the furbearers, Buffalo, Bear, and Beaver, are almost as numerous. The 25 buffalo names, with which are included *Boeuf Creek, Island,* and *Slough* in Franklin County, attest the day when the bison roamed over all the territory of the United States between the Alleghanies and the Rockies. There are 25 panther names, or "painter" as the pioneer called him, among them the *Isle of Panthers* in Lafayette County, and 20 for the related wildcat. The 50 wolf names include *Toad-a-Loop,* for Tour-de-loup, i.e., wolf's track, in Kansas City; and among the 15 otter names *Loutre Island* must not be omitted. There are 30 places named for the coon or raccoon, and 45 for the possum or opossum, including more than 15 "Possum Trots" or "Possum Walks."

Bear Creek (Marion), 1823
Beaver Lake (Wayne)
Boeuf Creek (Franklin)
Buck Mountain (Iron)
Buffalo (county seat of Dallas), 1841
Castor River (St. Francois to New Madrid)   (i.e., the beaver)
Coon Creek (Pettis)
Crane (Stone), 1895
Deerfield (Vernon), 1871
Doe Run (St. Francois), 1888
Eagleville (Harrison), 1881
Elkland (Webster), 1882
Elkton (Hickory), 1867
Fox River (Clark, etc)
Gopher Hill (Adair)
Isle of Panthers (Lafayette), 1804

Loutre Island (Montgomery and Warren)   (i.e., the otter)
Lupus (Moniteau)   (i.e., the wolf)
Otterville (Cooper), 1837
Panther Creek (Bates)   (formerly pronounced "Painter")
Possum Trot (Taney)
Rattlesnake Hollow (Reynolds)
SNAKE COUNTY (for McDonald before 1849)
Toad-a-Loop (Jackson)   (for Tour-de-Loup, i.e., wolf's track)
    (rocky bluffs near the Kaw River in the southwest part of
    Kansas City)
Wolf Island (Mississippi), 1792

NAMES OF APPROBATION AND DISAPPROBATION (26)

Disapprobation:
Deslet (Shannon), 1899   (meant for "Desolate")
Hardscrabble (Bates)
Hardscrabble School (Howell)
                    (now changed to Pleasant View School)
Lickskillet (Cass), 1840
Misere (old name for Ste. Genevieve)
Paincourt (old name for St. Louis), 1764
Slapout (Butler)
Smackout (Boone)
Solo (Texas)   (for a lonesome place)
Stinking Creek (Clark)   (now known as Fox River)
Approbation:
Fairmount (Henry), 1857
Florissant (St. Louis), 1785
La Belle (Lewis) 1857
Montebello (Jefferson), 1860
Pleasant Gap (Bates), 1840
Pleasant Green (Cooper), 1873
Pleasant Grove (Ripley), 1878
Pleasant Hill (Cass), 1865
Pleasant Home (Putnam)
Pleasant Hope (Polk)
Pleasanton (Mercer)—now in Iowa
Pleasant Retreat (Scotland), 1849
Pleasant View (Cedar)
Pleasantville (Sullivan), 1858
Queen City (Schuyler), 1867
Sweet Springs (Saline), 1838

Missourians have not always felt satisfied with their homes, if we may
judge by the place names they at first conferred upon them. They have
protested, though usually with a smile, against loneliness, poverty, and star-
vation when these evils came upon them. There was a time when "hungry
places" nearly filled the State—or at least when the intimation that their
neighbors were acquainted with such privations was a favorite piece of
pioneer humor.

Our ancestors seem to have thought it hilariously funny to suggest that nearby communities did not always have enough to eat, and hence that they were reduced to nature's method of extracting the last morsel from their cooking vessels. There are no fewer than 8 places in Missouri that once bore the mocking name of *Lickskillet*. Most of them have now exchanged their homely old name for something more "refined," for we no longer have a sense of humor quite so robust as did our fun-loving forefathers. Other "hungry names" once widely used were *Smackout, Slapout,* and *Hardscrabble*. Seven places in Missouri were once known as *Hardscrabble,* the most famous one being, as we have already mentioned, the name given by Gen. U. S. Grant to his log cabin near St. Louis where he lived from 1848 to 1859 and waged the stiffest battle of his entire career in a bitter struggle for his daily bread.

As for the name of *Slapout*, we have in our files a letter from Mr. W. N. Barron which tells exactly how the town in Butler County where he once lived acquired its "hungry name," before he persuaded them to change it to *Fagus:* "The railroad grading crew boarded at the only shack there. The crew would come in tired and hungry, and the proprietor would serve them a dish of beans and bread, always apologizing by saying that he would serve meat, only at that particular time he was 'slap out' of it. This happened at about every meal, with the result that the word became the name of the place."

St. Louis itself was once called *Paincourt,* i.e., "short of bread." The same ancient jest was responsible for such venerable British names as Coldharbour, i.e. "chilly fare or entertainment," and Starveacre. Our ancestors must have been fairly well fed as a rule, or they would hardly have considered the imputation of food shortage as quite so exquisitely amusing.

The oldest permanent settlement in Missouri, *Ste. Genevieve,* once went by the depressing name of *Misère,* which is matched by such later names chosen by the American settlers as *Solo* and *Deslet.* The early inhabitants of the last named place may not have been strong in the matter of spelling, but they knew how they felt about the place they lived in.

On the whole, however, Missourians have found their State a pleasant place, and they seem to have liked it better the longer they lived here. The 30 or 40 unfavorable names we have in our files are counterbalanced by more than ten times that number that express their satisfaction. The adjective "Pleasant" is by far the most frequently used term in making up the names on our map. We have computed the prodigious number of 403 separate places within the State which are acknowledged to be "Pleasant" by their names and are officially so listed in the index. There are in Missouri 24 Pleasant Views, 38 Pleasant Ridges, 55 Pleasant Valleys, 58 Pleasant Groves, 66 Mount Pleasants, and 82 Pleasant Hills. In these delectable spots there are found no fewer than 98 churches described as "Pleasant." More than that, we have 241 schools entitled "Pleasant." The idea that education ought to be made agreeable to the pupils is sometimes thought to be a modern innovation. Perhaps it was first discovered in Missouri.

None of these pleasant places, it is true, are large cities. Their inhabitants are evidently too much engaged in enjoying life to worry about growing too rapidly. But what a number of happy hamlets and contented villages we have scattered from one end of the State to the other, all the way from *Pleasant Gap* to *Pleasant View*. There is not a single place known as "Unpleasant" in the entire State.

There are some pleasant places, it is true, outside of Missouri. There are a few even in Great Britain; but the English Place-Name Society thinks that all these English names are probably ironical. Several Mount Pleasants, for example, in and around London were so called, it tells us, "from heaps of cinders or refuse that formerly occupied the sites." The English believe in taking their pleasures sadly.

In the rest of the United States, there are listed by Rand and McNally slightly over a hundred places known as "Pleasant" something or other, from Pleasant Bay in Maine to Pleasant Valley in California. But we have more than four times as many in our single State. Certainly no other commonwealth, so far as I have been able to discover, comes within hailing distance of Missouri in the sheer number of such genial and inviting place names. Perhaps we ought to alter the name of our State itself to Pleasance or Pleasantia or Pleasantina.

E. CULTURAL NAMES (285)

The last of our five main divisions of Missouri place names, which we have called Cultural, is the smallest, but in some respects the most interesting and revealing of them all. It reflects the aspirations and ideals of the people of the State, their literary and artistic interests, their religious inheritance, and their distinctive sense of humor. We have divided them into seven sub-sections, entitled Ideal Names, Literary Names, Classical Names, Bible Names, Saints' Names, Humorous Names, and Coined Names.

IDEAL NAMES (35)

Missourians have always had high ideals, and they have been especially fond of naming places for them. The ideal most widely commemorated has been *Liberty*. Such names as *Independence, Freedom, Liberal,* and *Fairplay* are scattered all over the State. Next to Liberty, we have always loved Union. Missouri is full of *Unities, Uniontowns,* and *Unionvilles, Concord* and *Harmony, Amity* and *Friendship, Loyalty* and what the Germans call *Frieden Gemeinde.* Close behind these two comes the spirit of *Enterprise,* expressed in such names as *Energy, Industry, Competition,* and *Progress,* leading on, as we devoutly hope, to *Prosperity* and *Success.* Some of these names, it must be confessed, smack somewhat of our well-known advertising or "Show Me" spirit, as in the health resorts that call themselves *Cureall* or *Eaudevie.* But if the old "Show Me State" can only live up to her place names, she will more than justify all that her complacent citizens can claim for her. The 35 such names listed below, selected as samples from more than 100, will at least show what we are aiming at.

Advance (Stoddard), 1910
Alliance (Bollinger), 1891
Amity (De Kalb), 1870
Apex (Lincoln), 1886
Clever (Christian), 1893
Competition (Laclede), 1867
Concord (Callaway), 1837
Concordia (Lafayette), 1868
Cureall (Howell), 1875
Eaudevie (Christian), 1904
Economy (Macon), 1837
Eldorado (Clark), 1853
Energy (Scotland), 1895
Enterprise (Shelby), 1886
Exchange (Reynolds), 1888
Fairplay (Miller) 1860
Freedom (Osage), 1890
Frieden Gemeinde (St. Charles), 1836
Friendship (Caldwell), 1879
Harmony Mission (Bates), 1821

Independence (county seat of Jackson), 1827
Industry (Henry), 1883
Liberal (Barton), 1881
Liberty (county seat of Clay), 1822
Loyalty (Laclede), 1918
Progress (Audrain)
Prosperine (Laclede), 1901
Prosperity (Jasper)
Success (Texas), 1883
Tranquility (Clark), 1902
Union (county seat of Franklin), 1827
Uniontown (Perry), about 1870
Unionville (county seat of Putnam), 1853
Unity (Scotland), 1876
Victory Hill (Butler), 1927

LITERARY NAMES (33)

The reading habits of Missourians are well reflected in their place names. They indicate that the two favorite authors among our people have always been Shakespeare and Sir Walter Scott. Shakespeare is represented by *Avon* and *Avondale, Elsinore, Portia*, and *Belmont*, Scott by *Waverley* and *Ivanhoe*. Other famous British writers have furnished their share: *Selma*, heroine of the Ossian poems ascribed to Macpherson; *Darien*, from a familiar sonnet by Keats; *Avalon*, from Tennyson's "Idylls of the King"; and *Flanders Cave*, from John McCrae's unforgettable "In Flanders Fields." From the Continent come *Concordia*, here listed again because its Lutheran founders took its name from a line in Schiller's "Lied von der Glocke" ("Concordia soll ihr Name sein"); *Undine*, from the German classic by De la Motte Fouqué; and *Fanchon*, heroine of George Sand's best loved French romance.

American literature is represented by Longfellow's *Wayside Inn*, his *Winona* in "Hiawatha," and his *Excelsior*, by Helen Hunt Jackson's *Ramona*, and by the *Mark Twain Cave* and *Memorial Bridge* at Hannibal to commemorate our own beloved Clemens. Popular best-sellers of their day, most of them now forgotten, are remembered at *Zanoni*, from Bulwer Lytton's novel of 1843; *East Lynne*, from Mrs. Henry Woods' favorite of 1861; *Elmo*, from Jane Evans Wilson's "St. Elmo" of 1866; *Burr Oaks*, from the setting of E. P. Roe's "Opening a Chestnut Burr" of 1874; *Ardath*, from Marie Corelli's novel of 1889; *Green Gables*, from "Anne of Green Gables," 1908, by Lucy Maud Montgomery; *Limberlost*, from "A Girl of the Limberlost," 1909, by Mrs. Gene Stratton Porter; and of course our own Harold Bell Wright at the *Shepherd of the Hills Estate*. There are even some place names like *Rinky Dink* and *Toonerville* which have been taken from the comic strips.

Ardath (Barton), 1910
Arden (Douglas), 1887

Arkoe (Nodaway), 1874
Avalon (Livingston), 1845
Avon (Cass), 1887
Avondale (Clay),1819
Belmont (Henry), 1855
Braggadocio (Pemiscot), 1847
Burr Oaks (Howell), 1936
Concordia (Lafayette), 1868
Darien (Dent), 1889
East Lynne (Cass), 1871
Elmo (Nodaway), 1879
Elsinore (Carter), 1889
Excelsior Springs (Clay), 1881
Fanchon (Howell), 1901
Flanders Cave (Miller), about 1920
Green Gables (Camden), 1915
Ivanhoe (Shelby), 1876
Limberlost (Crawford)
Mark Twain (or Tom Sawyer) Cave (Marion)
Mark Twain Memorial Bridge (Marion), 1935
Portia (Vernon), 1894
Ramona Park (St. Louis), before 1909
Rinky Dink Club House (Butler)
Selma (Jefferson), 1837
Shepherd of the Hills Estate (Taney)
Toonerville (St. Charles), 1904
Undine (Howell), 1870
Waverly (Lafayette), about 1870
Wayside Inn (Lewis), erected in 1835, but present title
    not conferred till after it had become a historic
    landmark
Winona (Shannon), 1889
Zanoni (Ozark), 1898

For two of these literary names there is more to be said. No name in the State has aroused more idle speculation than has *Braggadocio* down in Pemiscot County. All records of the exact circumstances of its naming seem to have been lost, and many stories have been invented of the familiar "ex post facto" type, as for example about the first settler's having been given to much boasting about the beauty of his wife, who had the remarkable name of "Docio"—in other words, "bragging on Docio." It need hardly be said that such feeble attempts at etymological wit are not to be taken too seriously.

Obviously, however, *Braggadocio* is a humorous name, chosen by some one in ridicule of the boastful or over-optimistic disposition of its earliest inhabitants. Missourians have never been backward in proclaiming the superlative merits of their great commonwealth. If they have a fault, it is perhaps just this tendency to be a trifle too voluble and vain-glorious about themselves; and their envious neighbors have not been slow to poke fun at this propensity. Our own "Son of Missouri," Mark Twain, satirized in classic fashion this type of Missourian in his immortal portrait of Colonel Mulberry Sellers in his *Gilded Age,* who was always discovering imaginary millions in Missouri mud-flats. Apparently Colonel Sellers had some spiritual ancestors in Pemiscot County.

There is a perfect parallel to the name of *Braggadocio* in that of *Gasconade County,* which was conferred long before by the witty French people of St. Louis upon the exuberant settlers in the region a little farther up the Missouri River. They are said on good authority to have conferred the name of *Gasconade* on the river and the region round about it because of the way its first settlers used to brag about their district when they visited St. Louis. The implication was that they resembled the Gascons, inhabitants of the province of Gascony back in France, who it seems have always been noted for their boastfulness.

The unknown jester who selected the name *Braggadocio* for the hopeful new settlement in Pemiscot found his name, not in French history, but in one of the great classics of English literature. There can be no doubt that he borrowed the name from Edmund Spenser's *Faerie Queen.* It was Spenser who first coined the name, in the Third Canto of his Second Book, for his famous comic character, that vain-glorious knight and horsethief Sir Braggadocchio. This rascal, Spenser tells us, was at the start merely "a losell wandering by the way," who

> in his kestrel kind
> A pleasing vein of glory vain did find,
> To which his flowing tongue and troublous spright
> Gave him great aid, and made him more inclined:
> He that brave steed there finding ready dight,
> Purloined both steed and spear, and fled away full light.

For quite some time this "four-flusher," as he would be called in our modern American slang, was taken at his own valuation by all those he met:

> Now gan his heart all swell in jollity,
> And of himself great hope and help conceived;
> That, puffed up with smoke of vanity,
> And with self-loved personage deceived,
> He gan to hope of men to be received
> For such as he him thought, or fain would be believed.

But his true worth was ignominiously exposed by a woman; for when he encountered the warlike lady knight Belphoebe, at the first sight of her

> he from his lofty steed
> Down fell to ground, and crept into a bush,
> To hide his coward head.

Spenser took great pains to devise just the right sobriquet for him, by welding the English word "brag" to the Italian suffix "-occhio" or "-occio," used for things swollen or inflated. He created a personification of empty-headed vanity over which his readers have been laughing ever since.

One Pemiscot County reader there must have been who laughed with him. He must have had access somehow to a first-class library, where he evidently read and loved the finest things in literature. More than that, he must have expected some at least of his neighbors to recognize his allusion. Not every Bostonian in those days, and not many of our college graduates today, know their Spenser as well as he did. I wish we knew his name. Probably there were a good many other Missourians like him. At any rate, when we are told, as we sometimes are by supercilious Eastern critics like Van Wyck Brooks, that early Missouri was a barren waste so far as culture or acquaintance with the classics was concerned, we can cite one pioneer gentleman in Missouri who was certainly an exception to the indictment.

The other literary name which calls for special comment is *Arkoe*. The name of this little village up in Nodaway County, near Maryville, gave us perhaps the longest and most exciting chase into place-name origins that we have ever had to make. The county records told us only that *Arkoe* was laid off and named in 1874 by a Dr. P. H. Talbot. Some of the present residents thought he had found the old name in Jules Verne's extremely popular romance, *Twenty Thousand Leagues under the Sea*. But we have learned that it is never safe to accept such local guesses at face value, if they are capable of verification. No such name appears in that or any other of Verne's famous stories.

Meanwhile, however, we did learn a good deal about the town's founder. Dr. Talbot was one of the most remarkable men Missouri has ever produced. He was a country physician and an extremely able man, cultured and widely read, with a notable library in his home at *Arkoe,* which he had named, out of Hawthorne, *"The House of Seven Gables."* He was also extremely active in the politics of that stormy period just after the Civil War, local, state, and national, making many enemies as well as friends. Eventually he was assassinated, while resting after his rounds in that very library of his *Arkoe* home, by a shot fired through one of its windows. And at the end of a sensational murder trial, it was one of his own sons who was convicted of the atrocious crime.

The mystery of the name he gave to his town has at last been solved, and its solution is connected with that famous library the doctor had in his *"House of Seven Gables."* One of the books on its shelves must have been an old classic of English literature, now almost forgotten, entitled *Peter Wilkins and the Flying Indians,* written by Robert Paltock back in the eighteenth century. *Peter Wilkins,* though little read nowadays, is a real classic. It is one of the best of the great series of imaginary voyages written in the age of Swift and Defoe.

Readers of Paltock's absorbing adventure story, which delighted Lamb and Coleridge, will well remember his "Flying Indians." They anticipated in amazingly prophetic fashion the methods of the modern airman. It was their custom, Paltock tells us, to take off and land on water, just as hydroplanes do today. Suitable stretches of water for landing on were called by these fictitious Indians, in the imaginary language which the ingenious author invented for them, by the name of "arkoes."

Now it happens that Dr. Talbot's town stands on the banks of the broad and placid stream known as the *One Hundred and Two · River*—another mysterious name, by the way, for which we have attempted a solution on another page. There can be little doubt that the doctor must have recently finished reading his *Peter Wilkins* when he chose his name for the town he had just founded. He must have seen in his mind's eye those flying Indians rising and descending on the water right outside his library windows. Perhaps he even had a vision of Paltock's beautiful winged maiden Youwarkee, one of the most charming heroines in all fiction, gracefully alighting on the *One Hundred and Two*, out there just beyond his reach.

There is a quaint old eighteenth century engraving in one of the early editions of *Peter Wilkins* that depicts Youwarkee arising from the water. Beside it might be placed a modern airplane photograph of Nodaway County which I have seen. It clearly reveals just what a perfect "arkoe" *Arkoe* is.

Our old-time Missourians may have led violent lives, just as the Elizabethans did. But surely no one has the right to accuse them, as Brooks has done in his *Ordeal of Mark Twain*, of being uncultured, unlettered, and unimaginative.

CLASSICAL NAMES (30)

Some of the Missourians of older days knew their Greek and Roman classics quite familiarly, certainly much better than do most of the products turned out by our so-called "modern education." The Jasper County Court which resolved, on March 29, 1842, that their new town should be named for the ancient city of. *Carthage;* the Pike County surveyor Frank Meriwether in 1886 who called the town he had just laid out *Eolia,* for Aeolus, the God of Wind, because, as he said, it was one of the windiest days he had ever seen; the proprietor of a large apple orchard in Howell County in 1895 who chose the name of *Pomona,* the goddess of fruits, for his new foundation because it was situated in such a good fruit section; the postmaster in Wright County in 1889 who asked for the name of *Omega* because his was the last post office at that time to be established in the county; or Mr. Crumb, who built the railroad in Stoddard County in 1910 and named the station his line had just reached *Zeta,* "because he was interested in all things classical" and just at that time was especially interested in learning how to make the sixth letter of the Greek alphabet—none of these Missourians dreamed that the day would ever come when the study of Greek and Latin would become almost obsolete in our schools and colleges.

Perhaps the most striking and authentic instance of the selection of a classical name and the motives that prompted it is provided in the case of *Herculaneum* in Jefferson County. That town was laid out in 1808 by Moses Austin, the great lead miner of Jefferson and Washington Counties, and the father of a still more remarkable son, Stephen Fuller Austin, who later became the "Father of the State of Texas." For his new mining center on the banks of the Mississippi, Moses Austin chose the name of the ancient Roman town that was buried by Mount Vesuvius under sixty feet of lava in the year 79 A.D. That old town was just being unearthed again during the latter part of the eighteenth century, and a flood of books about its incredible treasures was pouring from the press. Moses Austin had a well-stocked library at *Durham Hall,* his mansion in Washington County. No doubt it contained a copy of Bellicard's *Antiquities of Herculaneum* of 1753, with its 42 plates engraved by the author, or else of Maréchal's twelve-volume work issued from 1780 to 1803, with its magnificent engravings by David. We can still pore over these fascinating volumes today, and can easily understand the idea that must have come to him. He is said to have selected the name of *Herculaneum* because the poisonous smoke from his own lead smelters reminded him of the smoke that once rose from Mount Vesuvius, and also because he fancied that the edges of the limestone strata along the Mississippi resembled the seats of the great amphitheatre recently uncovered in the old Italian city.

Here are 30 of Missouri's classical place names, selected from a list several times as long:

Alexandria (Clark), 1848
Arbela (Scotland), 1860
Arcadia (Iron), 1849
Argo (Crawford), 1853
Athens (Gentry), 1845
Aurora (Lawrence), 1870
Carthage (Jasper), 1842
Corcyra (Morgan), 1901
Eolia (Pike), 1886
Fabius River (Marion, etc.)
Halcyon (Dent), 1904
Hannibal (Marion), 1819
Herculaneum (Jefferson), 1808
Ionia (Benton), 1882
"New Thermopylae," 1843 (Dickens' name for
              Hannibal in "Martin Chuzzlewit")
Omega (Wright), 1889

Osiris (Cedar), 1900
Ovid (Ray), 1889
Palmyra (county seat of Marion), 1819
Plato (Texas), 1874
Pomona (Howell) 1895
Port Scipio (Marion), 1825
Samos (Mississippi), 1910
Tigris (Douglas)) 1921
Troy (county seat of Lincoln), 1825
Viginti (Clay), before 1880
    (the old name of Excelsior Springs, because of the
    20 mineral springs it then had)
Vulcan (Iron), 1915
Zephyr (Bollinger), 1910
Zeta (Stoddard), 1910
Zodiac (Vernon), 1881

A knotty problem has arisen in connection with the remarkable cluster of classically named places in Marion County: *Fabius, Scipio, Hannibal,* and *Palmyra.* It has been exhaustively and faithfully dealt with in Miss Katherine Elliott's fine thesis of 1938 on the "Place Names of Six Northeast Counties." Here her conclusions, which seem to be amply justified, may be briefly summarized.

An apocryphal story was related in 1884 by R. I. Holcombe in his *History of Marion County,* which has been many times repeated without investigation, although Holcombe himself later disavowed it. According to this unfounded anecdote, the three names of *Hannibal, Scipio,* and *Fabius* were first conferred by Don Antonio Soulard, the last Spanish Surveyor-General. Holcombe originally wrote:

> Don Antonio was a great admirer of some of the characters
> of Roman and Carthaginian history, and on his first voyage up
> the Mississippi, somewhere about 1800, he christened a number of
> the streams after some of those ancient heroes.

He goes on to say that Soulard gave the name of *Hannibal* to Bear Creek, on which the present city of *Hannibal* (which was not founded till 1819) now stands; that he rechristened *Bay de Charles* as the *Scipio River,* in honor of Scipio Africanus, who conquered Hannibal; and that then he named the *Fabius River* for Fabius Maximus, the Roman general so skilful in retreat.

But as Miss Elliott convincingly demonstrates, there is no authority whatever for the existence of any of the three classical names prior to the founding of *Hannibal* in 1819, which took place after Soulard's death. Nor was it the habit of the French or Spanish to resort to classical history for any of the places they are known to have named. On the other hand, the adoption of classical names was a marked characteristic of the later American settlers. She quotes from Miss Cooper, daughter of James Fenimore Cooper, to this effect:

> After the Revolution came the direful invasion of the ghosts of old Greeks and Romans, headed by the Yankee Schoolmaster with an Abridgement of Ancient History in his pocket. It was then your Romes and Palmyras, your Homers and Virgils, were dropped about the country in scores.

Doubtless, thinks Miss Elliott, *Hannibal* and the other two names were proposed by some classically minded settler, perhaps by the same man who instigated, that same year, the name of *Hannibal's* great rival, *Palmyra*, which has never been ascribed to Soulard. William V. Rector, the American Surveyor-General, who had an important part in the founding of *Hannibal*, might have done it, or Colonel William Muldrow or the Rev. Ezra Stiles Ely, or any of their associates, fired by the same spirit that led to the ambitious planning of that center of classical learning that was christened under the name of *Marion College* in 1831.

Miss Eliott makes the very plausible suggestion that this whole Marion County constellation of classical names arose by a mere misunderstanding, or perhaps a deliberate alteration, of the original name of the *Fabius River*. That name, as we have seen above, was never written as *Fabius* until 1834. Before that year it appears as "R. Fabiane" on the Lewis and Clark Map of 1809, and as "Ferbien" on a later map of 1822. Most likely it was named for some one of those forgotten French traders and trappers who have left their imprint so widely on Missouri nomenclature. Then when *Hannibal* was founded, it occurred to some antiquarian-minded American that Fabiane or Ferbien sounded somewhat like Fabius; and with that as his starting-point, he proceeded to invent the names *Hannibal* and *Scipio* to go with it. Whoever he was, he has been too modest to bequeath his own name to us.

George R. Stewart, in his *Names on the Land*, provides a perfect parallel to our conjecture about the *Fabius* in the origin of the name of *Lake Seneca* in New York. That came from the name of an Indian tribe which the Dutch wrote down as "Sinneken." Then some classically schooled Englishman noticed that it looked like the name of the famous Roman philosopher Seneca; and *Seneca* it has been ever since. Probably, says Stewart, it was from *Lake Seneca* that the board of commissioners appointed in 1790 to select names for 25 townships in western New York got the inspiration for the well-known "classical belt" of names in that State. But New York was certainly no more classically minded at that time than Missouri.

As Professor Stewart writes in concluding his discussion of this whole matter of American classical names (p. 187):

> The classical interests of the later eighteenth century are as

much part of the history of the United States as the existence of the Indian tribes or the Revolution. To maintain, as many have done, that Rome and Troy are mere excrescences on our map, is to commit the fallacy of denying one part of history in favor of another part—or else to be ignorant of history.

The ideals and aspirations of the Americans of that period deserve their perpetuation.

BIBLE NAMES (52)

One classic that Missourians assuredly once knew well, and some of them have not entirely forgotten even today, is the Bible. Our Bible place names outnumber those that come from all other books combined; and if we had space to list all the churches and schools with Scriptural names, the total would be increased five or six fold. Many of the towns with such names borrowed them from earlier churches in their neighborhoods; but by no means all the Bible names came from churches. Almost all the familiar spots of the Holy Land have been transplanted to Missouri soil. The Hebrews of the Old Testament described the whole compass of their little country as stretching "from Dan to Beersheba." Here in Missouri one can journey from *Dan,* in Maries County, to *Beersheba* only a few miles away in Montgomery. We can follow all the steps of Abraham, of the Gospels, and the missionary journeys of Paul on our Missouri map without missing a single one of them.

Our forefathers knew their Bibles better than we do. One wonders if the most assiduous Bible student today could locate *Enon* and *Minnith,* or identfiy *Ava* or *Ulam,* without using a concordance. They searched the Scriptures from end to end, and did not overlook places or persons never mentioned but once in its pages. Sometimes their interpretations of the sacred text seem to us a bit cryptic, not to say captious. *Enon* was always a popular name for churches or towns on the waterside, for reasons that elude us until we read the account of John the Baptist in John 3:23: "And John also was baptizing in Aenon near to Salim, because there was much water there." The use of *Minnith* for a town which it was hoped would be a grain center is explained by a verse in Ezekiel 27-17: "They traded in the market wheat of Minnith." Proper names were often allegorized according to their supposed meanings. Thus *Ulam,* who is mentioned only once (1 Chronicles 7:16) as a grandson of Manasseh, was thought to mean "solitary." Apparently the founder of *Ulam,* Missouri, meant to intimate that his town was a solitary place. He might be comforted to know that according to the latest Biblical interpreters the name really meant "foremost," if in the meantime his village had not unfortunately disappeared from the map altogether.

The most original example of allegorical methods is provided by the name of *Ava,* the county seat of Douglas. We are told in II Kings 17:24 that it was a heathen city which took a leading part in the oppression of the Chosen People: "And the king of Assyria brought men from Ava . . . and placed them in the cities of Samaria instead of the children of Israel; and they possessed Samaria, and dwelt in the cities thereof." *Ava* is supposed to mean "overthrowing." Apparently its founder intended a humorous reference to Ava's "overthrowing" its rival aspirant for the county seat. If one story told down in Douglas County is true, the overthrow was not accomplished in strict accordance with Scriptural rules of behavior. It is alleged that the three commissioners appointed to lay out the town stole the county records from its hated rival *Vera Cruz* and brought them over to *Ava* by force, thus establishing their town as the official head of the county permanently.

Some such reasons may account for the rather surprising use made of the names of the cities of the Philistines, *Gath* and *Ascalon,* or of the town of *Sodom,* which Scripture tells us was so wicked that it had to be destroyed by fire sent down from heaven. Such derogatory names were sometimes conferred on a place by its neighbors. Our *Sodom* down in Dade County, we are told, was so called because it was such a "wild, rough place." One is glad to learn that it has since changed its name, and it is to be hoped its nature as well. No Gomorrhah has so far been discovered in Missouri.

Antioch (Clark), 1886
Aquilla (Stoddard)—by error for Aquila
Ascalon (St. Louis), 1897
Ava (county seat of Douglas), 1871
Beersheba (Montgomery), 1888
Bethany (county seat of Harrison), 1845
Bethel (Shelby), 1848
Bethlehem (Montgomery), 1886
Bethpage (McDonald), about 1885
Boaz (Christian), 1900
Canaan (Gasconade), 1840
Corinth (Phelps)
Cyrene (Pike)
Damascus (St. Clair), 1896
Dan (Maries), 1901
Dothan (Atchison), 1880
Eden (Dent), 1886
Elim (Shelby), 1845
Emmaus Creek (Warren)
Enon (Moniteau)
Gath (Johnson)
Gilead (Lewis), 1860
Haggai (St. Francois), 1890

Hebron (Douglas), 1904
Iconium (St. Clair), 1879
Ishmael (Washington), 1930
Jacob's Well (Franklin), 1863
Jericho (Laclede), 1867
Jerusalem (Lewis, also Cedar), 1840
Jordan Creek (Franklin, also Cedar)
Lebanon (county seat of Laclede), 1853
Macedonia (Phelps), 1891
Mamre (Shelby), 1848
Minnith (Ste. Genevieve), 1886
Moab (Pulaski), 1891
Mount Carmel (Audrain), 1932
Mount Moriah (Harrison), 1856
Mount Nebo (Crawford)
Mount Zion   Church (Boone)
      (site of a bloody battle during the Civil War)
Naomi (Marion), 1876
Nebo (Laclede), 1870
Nineveh (Lincoln), 1844
Palestine (Laclede), 1889
Pisgah (Cooper), 1830
Salem (county seat of Dent), 1853
Shibboleth (Washington), 1798 (sic)
Shiloh (Butler), 1874
Siloam Springs (Howell), before 1880
Sodom (Dade), 1840 (now known as Finley or Dildy Mill)
Ulam (Ste. Genevieve), 1890
Zion (Madison), 1886
Zoar (Gasconade), 1899

SAINTS' NAMES (31)

Ireland has long been known as the Island of the Saints; but Missouri, if judged by its place names, might well claim the proud title of the Saintly State. No fewer than 500 names in our files are derived directly or indirectly from the saints of the church. Most of them, naturally, are names of churches, schools, or asylums; but also included are the names of five Missouri rivers or bayous, four of our oldest counties, and at least 50 towns, ranging all the way from the cities of St. Louis, St. Charles, and St. Joseph to a goodly host of smaller but thriving towns and villages.

Sometimes the name was chosen because the place happened to be founded on a particular saint's day, the day of the year, that is, traditionally fixed as that of his or her death or martyrdom. Such may have been the case, though here no certainty is available, with *Ste. Genevieve*, the oldest white settlement in the State, if the first landing there took place as it may have done on or about Jan. 3, 1735.

Places were seldom named directly for living persons by the French or Spanish, as was so often done by the more frankly egotistic Anglo-Saxons. Thus *St. Louis* was not named, as is sometimes mistakenly asserted, for Louis XV of France, or *St. Charles* for Charles III or VI of Spain, for these royal personages were anything but saints themselves. Instead they were dedicated to their name-saints, the devout and gallant St. Louis IX and the beloved and eloquent St. Charles Borromeo. So when *St. Joseph* was founded in 1840 by Joseph Robidoux, and when it was first proposed to name it Robidoux, the sturdy old pioneer modestly preferred to dedicate his town to his celestial patron. In the same way *St. James* in Phelps County honors St. James the Apostle directly, but indirectly also Thomas James, its founder, who was a devout Episcopalian; *St. Martha* in Lawrence was so named for Mrs. Martha Wild by her husband William R. Wild, who laid it out; and *St. Anna* in Texas County by Bob Williams in memory of his wife, Mrs. Anna Williams, who had just died. *St. Johns* in Franklin County probably got its name from old *Fort San Juan del Misuri*, which was built by the Spaniards before 1796 somewhere on the river in what is now either Franklin or Warren County, and the fort honored indirectly the famous Don Juan of Austria (1547-1578), the victor at Lepanto.

Over 100 saints have thus been honored in the names of Missouri places, churches, or institutions. St. Joseph apparently leads all the rest, with over forty, but close behind him are St. John the Apostle and St. Mary the Virgin, each with thirty or more.

St. Anna (Texas), 1910
St. Aubert (Callaway), 1848 (now vanished)
St. Aubert (Osage), 1855
St. Charles, 1769
St. CHARLES COUNTY, 1812
St. Clement (Pike), 1870
St. Elizabeth (Miller), 1875
St. Francis River; before 1821
Saint Francisville (Clark), 1835
St. FRANCOIS COUNTY, 1821
Ste. Genevieve, 1735
Ste. GENEVIEVE COUNTY, 1812
St. James (Phelps), 1860
St. James River (or James River) (Stone)
St. John (Putnam) 1846
St. Johns (Franklin), before 1796
St. Johns Bayou (New Madrid), 1815
St. Joseph (Buchanan), 1840
St. Laurent's (or Lora) Creek (Ste. Genevieve)
St. Louis, 1764
St. LOUIS COUNTY, 1812
St. Louis University (St. Louis), 1818

St. **Luke** (Webster), 1846
St. **Martha** (Lawrence), 1870
St. **Mary** (St. Genevieve), 1818
St. **Mary's River, and Lake St. Mary** (New Madrid)
  (both of these were destroyed in the earthquakes
  of 1811-1812)
St. **Patrick** (Clark), 1876
St. **Paul** (St. Charles), 1866
St. **Peters** (St. Charles), 1853
St. **Thomas** (Cole), 1855

OTHER RELIGIOUS NAMES (18)

Religion has been pervasive in all of Missouri's life and history. Its influence has been abundantly evident in every one of our previous categories of Missouri place names, particularly, of course, in the two lists just given of Bible and saints' names. But there remain some additional names of great social and historic interest which have had religious origins and which do not fit into any of the special groups or sub-groups already listed. They are names that sprang from the particular traditions and personalities that have played vital parts in Missouri's many and varied denominations and religious movements.

For some of these special sects and groups there are certain distinctive key-words that have stamped themselves upon many of our place names. The use of the name *Westminster* marks any church or institution as probably Presbyterian, because its standards of faith and government were drawn up at the famous Westminster Assembly of 1643-1649. In the same way, *Epworth* is almost synonymous with Methodism, because its founder John Wesley (1703-1791) was born at the little village of Epworth in England.

Just so the name of *Dover* is a special favorite with both the Baptist and the Christian denomination. There are at least six Dover Churches in the State, four of them Baptist, including the very old one in Lewis County, and two Christian, including the famous old *Dover Church* in Lafayette County, said to be the oldest of that denomination in the State. There are seven *Dover Schools*, two *Dover Townships*, and two towns named *Dover*, almost all of which are known to have transferred their names from neighboring churches. All our Dovers seem to have their ultimate explanation in the career of that remarkable man Alexander Campbell (1788-1866), the founder of the Disciples movement. He began as a Presbyterian, but seceded from that denomination and joined the Baptists in 1812. Among them he proved a storm center of controversy in Ohio, Pennsylvania, and Virginia. One after another of the Baptist "Associations" in those States was disrupted by his new teachings, and either expelled Campbell and his followers, or else followed him out of the Baptist Church. The climax came in 1832 with the celebrated "Dover Association Report," issued by the Dover Association of Virginia, one of the oldest and strongest of the Baptist regional divisions. It was a vigorous declaration in favor of complete severance. The decree was carried into effect, and nearly half of the churches in the Dover Association decided to secede along with Campbell.

After the schism, and perhaps partly as a result of the deep feelings which it had aroused on either side, both the Baptists and the new "Christian" body began a remarkable period of expansion in the Middle West, which soon put them, along with the Methodists, far in the lead in point of numbers among all Protestant denominations in that part of the country. Probably as a result of these events, the name of *Dover* became a sort of watchword with both religious bodies. To the Christians it came to symbolize their birth, to the Baptists their purification.

In much the same way, the name of *Concordia* has become a symbol of Lutheranism. Lutheran churches have been so entitled at Kirkwood and Maplewood in St. Louis County, and at many other places, as have Lutheran schools and colleges, and likewise the town of *Concordia* in Lafayette County, so named in 1868 by a Lutheran minister. He is said to have taken the name, as we have seen above, from a line of Schiller. But it hardly seems likely that its special association with Lutheranism could have arisen merely from a single passage, even in so great a poet as Schiller.

Perhaps the true explanation may be found in the history of that famous old school in St. Louis that bears the name of *Concordia Seminary*, the oldest Lutheran institution of higher learning in Missouri. Brought to St. Louis in 1849, it had been founded ten years before in Perry County, in the very year of the settlement there of the Saxon immigrants. The historic log cabin which was its earliest home is still preserved at *Altenberg*, where the devoted little colony passed through stormy and difficult days.

Whether it was called Concordia before it came to St. Louis we do not know. But it was on the hearts and minds of the Saxons before they ever left Germany to find a land where they could practise in perfect freedom the faith they held so ardently. Back in Dresden, the prospective pilgrims used to hold "Concordia-hours"—so called because their chief subject for discussion and meditation was the Lutheran "Formula of Concord." The reference is to the Confession of Faith adopted by the Evangelical Lutheran Church back in 1580, which is sometimes known in brief as the "Concordia." So the beloved name must have been far older than the Perry County settlement of 1839, or the poetry of Schiller. Its distinctive Lutheran associations go back to the very foundations of the denomination.

The dramatic story of the Saxon Migration of 1839 has been told in full by W. O. Forster in his "Settlement of the Saxon Lutherans," a dissertation written at Washington University in 1942. It has been called the "advance guard of German immigration to the West." The place names they brought with them from Saxony, of which the chief ones are *Altenburg, Wittenberg,* and *Frohna,* have already been discussed in our section on foreign borrowings. The career of their ill-fated leader, Pastor Martin Stephan, and his tragic downfall would make a moving study in religious psychology, which there is no space here to recapitulate. Two place names which may or may not have ever existed are alleged to have borne the name of the fallen leader. *Stephansburg* is said to have been the name he planned for his capital. It may have been the settlement later called *Dresden,* which has now disappeared from the map. The other was *Stephan's Landing* on the Mississippi River, where he actually disembarked in 1838, but it bore that name only for a few brief weeks. After his trial and deposition, when he was banished across the Mississippi and left to his fate on the Illinois side at the foot of a grotesque rock with the highly appropriate name, as it must have seemed to the horrified Saxons, of the *Devil's Bake-Oven,* the name of his Landing was changed to *Wittenberg.* His enemies have also charged that he intended to call the institution afterwards known as *Concordia Seminary* by the name of *Stephan's College.*

Another dynamic religious leader who came from Germany to Missouri about ten years later was Dr. William Keil. The *Bethel Community* which he planted in Shelby County in 1845 was one of the most remarkable and successful of the many communistic settlements that were set up on American soil during that period. At one time it numbered more than 1000 persons, and it flourished till 1855, when Keil left Missouri for Oregon, taking about 250 members of his community with him. He died in 1877, and his community was finally dissolved in 1879. Dr. Keil took the names of the various settlements he organized from the Old Testament: *Bethel, Mamre,* and *Hebron* in Shelby County and *Nineveh* in Adair County, all of which have been listed above under our Bible Names. The first and principal building erected by his community, at Bethel in 1848, was the *Old Colony Church.* It was the crowning work of these industrious people from an architectural point of view. Built of brick and stone after the type of churches in the Fatherland, it could accommodate more than 1000 people, and it was long the pride of the colonists and of the entire county as well.

The most sensational leader of a new religious movement in Missouri was that remarkable character who founded the Mormon faith, the Prophet Joseph Smith. His new religion had a stormy experience in our State. After his expulsion with all his followers from Jackson County in 1833, some of them went south into Bates County, where they are still remembered in the name of *Mormon Fork* or Creek. Most of them, however, followed him northward into Clay and then into what are now Caldwell and Daviess Counties, where they settled down for a short time in 1838. Then followed the Mormon War, one of the chapters of Missouri history which we have least cause to remember with pride, and the entire community was driven out of Missouri altogether into Illinois. There in 1840 the Prophet built and named the imposing city of *Nauvoo*, which was just across the Mississippi River from Clark County. Part of the town of *Memphis* in Scotland County west of Clark was long known by the name of the Mormon city. Of the subsequent events, the Prophet's death at the hands of a mob and the final expulsion in 1846 of his people from *Nauvoo* to begin their long trek across Iowa and the Great Plains, till at last they found a permanent home in Utah, it is unnecessary to speak, for these developments removed them from any further close proximity to Missouri.

These things explain why the Mormons left so few place names on Missouri soil. And yet the Prophet was a prolific coiner of new names. All his life he exercised the "gift of tongues" that was bestowed upon him when he first deciphered the "golden plates," by pouring forth strange and curious coinages such as Nauvoo and Deseret and the word Mormon itself, for which he alone could supply the meaning, and not even he the etymology. Many of his fantastic word-creations have found a place on the map. They have proved viable, which is more than can be said of a good many other names constructed according to all the orthodox rules of derivation. Joseph Smith deserves, indeed, to have a place in that extremely small class of word-makers who have successfully created words out of nothing, as Von Helmont did with the word "gas," Eastman with "kodak," and Lewis Carroll with his "chortle" and "snark" and "jabberwock."

One of his most impressive coinages was the name he conferred on the little Mormon village which he founded in Daviess County and baptized with the resounding title of *Adam-Ondi-Ahman*. In his amazing *Autobiography*, he records that on May 9, 1838, he led his followers across Grand River and selected a site for what he meant to be his future city. "The brethren called it Spring Hill," he writes, "but by the mouth of the Lord it was named Adam-Ondi-Ahman." It was there, he told them, that Adam, the "Ancient of Days," had come long before, just after he too had been expelled from the Garden of Eden, which was really located within the precincts of the present town of *Independence;* there Adam had lived and died; and in that same valley, just three and one half miles northwest of *Gallatin*, he will come again some day to meet with his posterity.

The little Mormon settlement there soon shortened the spelling of Smith's long name to *Di-amon, Diamong,* or *Diamond.* When they were expelled from Missouri entirely, their irreverent successors changed its name to *Cravensville*. Today all that is left on its site is a single log cabin. But a monument has recently been erected by returning visitors of the much persecuted sect on that lonely hillside, which is still known locally as *Adam's Grave*.

When Mark Twain wrote his *Innocents Abroad,* he told in one of the most amusing chapters how he had sought throughout Palestine for the tomb of Adam, in order that he might erect an appropriate tombstone over it. Had he known all the treasures of his native State, he might have spared himself the labor of journeying so far to weep over the sepulchre of his earliest ancestor. Apparently he was quite unaware that the historic spot had already been identified and located in his own Missouri.

Many and beautiful are the names connected with the special objects or personages of Catholic veneration, as we have seen abundantly illustrated in the list of saints' names given just above. One saint whom Catholics have always revered, but who is practically unknown to most Protestants today, is St. Joachim. That is because he is not mentioned anywhere in the canonical books of Scripture, but only in the Apocrypha, which Protestants reject entirely and hardly ever read. It was not so in the days before the Reformation. The widespread use of St. Joachim's name both as a place name and as a surname in France, Germany, and Russia is due to that picturesque narrative in the Apocrypha entitled "Susanna and the Elders," which was enormously popular in the Middle Ages, and which has been called the earliest of all detective stories. Joachim was Susanna's husband, who loyally stood by her when she was falsely accused of adultery, until she was triumphantly vindicated by the shrewd detective methods of the righteous judge Daniel.

It happens that there are no places in Missouri directly named for the saint himself, which is the reason we have not included him in the preceding list. But there are many such places in Europe, the most famous being Joachimsthal in Bohemia, the original home of the almighty dollar. That fact alone should invest its name with special interest for Americans.

From the rich silver mine in the Bohemian Joachimsthal, discovered in 1516, were made the first dollars in the world. These big silver coins were first called "Joachimsthalers," then more briefly "thalers." In Low German mouths the word became "daler," and when the Dutch brought it over to America, it was transferred to the Spanish silver "pieces of eight" so much admired and coveted by the American colonists. Finally in 1785, in the Americanized spelling "dollar," it was adopted by the Continental Congress as the basic unit of our currency.

When General Patton's troops reached Bohemia during the late war, some of our American soldiers who had heard where our dollars came from, are reported to have searched the old valley, hoping to find there a hoard of the original Joachimsthalers. Had they only known it, they might have found an even richer treasure-trove in the valley of our own Missouri *Joachim* in Jefferson County.

That beautiful stream, probably named not directly for the saint, but for some early French settler who got his surname from him, is regularly pronounced and often spelled down there as *Swashin* or *Swashing Creek,* which is merely an Americanizèd approximation of the French pronunciation of the saint's name. Among our German immigrants, who were equally fond of the surname, it is pronounced in German fashion more nearly as Yoakum or Yocum. Thus we have *Yoakum's Mill* and *Yocum School* in Greene County, *Yochum Pond* in Stone, *Yokum School* in Wayne, *Yocum Branch* in Cass, and a hamlet called *Yocum* in Bates—all named for early settlers who tried to spell their ancient family name in the way that Americans could most easily apprehend it. Who but a plodding etymologist would ever suspect that the name of *Swashing Creek,* which empties into the Mississippi near *Herculaneum,* and that of *Yocum Branch* on the other side of the State, are really identical in origin?

Adam-Ondi-Ahman (Daviess), 1838
Adam's Grave (Daviess)
Christian College at Columbia (Boone), chartered in 1851
Concordia Seminary (St. Louis), 1849
Dover (Lafayette), 1839
Dover Christian Church (Lafayette), about 1832
Dover Baptist Church (Lewis), 1834
Epworth (Shelby), 1892
Epworth Hills (Iron)
Mormon Fork or Creek (Bates), after 1833
Nauvoo (Scotland), 1865
Old Colony Church (Shelby), 1848
Stephansburg (Perry), 1838
Stephan's Landing (Perry), 1838
Swashing (or Joachim) Creek (Jefferson)
Westminster College in Fulton (Callaway), 1853
Yoakum's Mill (Greene)
Yocum Branch (Cass)

HUMOROUS NAMES (48)

Missouri would not be the State that has produced America's greatest humorist if her people had not possessed and exhibited at all stages of her history a keen sense of humor. That quality of mind and heart is nowhere more abundantly exemplified than in her place names. Certainly there is an extraordinary number of humorous place names in the State; and what is truly remarkable, there are more of these humorous names in the northeast corner, the early home of Mark Twain, than anywhere else. Can that fact be merely a coincidence? Miss Elliott, in her thesis on "Six Northeast Counties," found no fewer than 135 names in and around Hannibal that originated in jest and mockery of one sort or another; and some of these embalmed and ancient jokes are amazingly like the jokes that were later coined by Hannibal's best known citizen, and about as good. Truly Mark Twain was a real "son of Missouri," sprung from its soil and of its earth earthy. Had he been born anywhere else he would assuredly have been a duller or at least a soberer man.

There are plenty of humorous names in other parts of the State also, and some of the best examples of Missouri wit have already been mentioned: the mocking epithets used by the French for many of their original settlements, such as *Paincourt, Vide Poche, Misère,* and *Gasconade;* the even cleverer hits scored by later American settlers in such names as *Braggadocio, Buncombe,* and *Pacific;* and the many "hungry names" scattered all over the State such as *Hardscrabble, Lickskillet, Smackout,* and *Slapout.* When Dickens visited us, he fell into our familiar Missouri habit of satirizing our own occasional grandiloquence by coining the fictitious name *"New Thermopylae"* for *Hannibal* and *"Eden"* for *Marion City;* and Mark Twain followed suit by calling *Marion City "Napoleon"* and *Palmyra "Constantinople."* Our local humorists have often done the same thing, as when they rechristened the little place with the big name of *Eldorado* as *Jimtown,* and *Maplewood* as *Pulltight.* We have a profusion of such comical nicknames, which are often better known and more used than are the real names. *Blackfoot* is the name still used in Boone County for the township of *Perche,* because of a report that the boys and girls of that region occasionally danced barefoot; *Buzzard's Roost* was the name bestowed upon the first tavern to be opened in Franklin County; and *Bachelor Creek* in that same county is still the name of the little stream where once lived a band of brave men who stubbornly refused to be led to the altar. A little place in Pemiscot is ironically known as *Who'd-a-Thought-It.* Especially do the nicknames in use for some of our schools sound as if they had been conferred by Tom Sawyer or Huckleberry Finn: *Buzzard's Glory, Devil's Hall, Jesse James School* (all given because these schools were located in rather "wild places"); *Brush College, Grubb College, Hoop Pole College,* and *Runt's Corner* (for little schools that were "down in the brush"); *Mustang School, Heelstring School, Hard Scratch School* (because the pupils had to climb a steep bluff to reach it); and *Cracker-Neck School* (because it stood on a hill where the view invited them to stretch their necks). In Franklin County, *Reed's Defeat* was the name somewhat unkindly given to a rural schoolhouse where the first teacher, a man named Reed, had life made so miserable for him by the big boys that the directors finally had to discharge him. Even churches were sometimes known by irreverent nicknames, such as *Old Rooster Church*

(from its weathervane), and *Old Ironsides Church* (from its staunch con-
servatism). These remind us of the name Mark Twain invented for Tom
Sawyer's church, *"Old Ship of Zion."*

Much has been written about the place names in Bret Harte's stories,
the characteristic names given to the mining camps of California by the gay
and reckless "Forty-Niners": Poker Flat and Sandy Bar, Red Dog and
Roaring Camp. Perhaps those Californians brought their picturesque nomenclature from Missouri. Long before 1849, the Missouri boatmen along
Loutre Slough had such names as *Slingtown,* so called for the "ginslings"
that were among their favorite drinks; *Gunboat,* for a rowdy saloon; and
Gore, for the red liquor it had on tap. Still earlier, reaching back even into
the eighteenth century, the lead miners of St. Francois, Crawford, and
Washington Counties liked to confer upon their "diggings" such names as
Skintown and *Shake Rag Hollow, Whisky Diggins* and *Crowbar Shaft, Jay
Bird Town* and *Mine Astraddle.* There was even a *Poker Hollow,* a *Poverty
Flat,* and a *Pucky-Huddle* among them. Life must have been fast and furi-
ous in Missouri in those days, to judge by their place names, even though
they mined mostly lead instead of gold. Had only a Bret Harte arisen
among us then, with a sharp eye for the colorful and the picturesque, we
Missourians might have laid claim to all the reflected romance that later
came to be associated with the "Wild West" of California, Montana, and
Colorado.

Another example of local dialect used in one of our early place names is
King Bee, adopted by a town in Ripley County that hoped to become the
most important place in the county. The term is not found as yet in any of
our dialect dictionaries. But Mark Twain knew its meaning when he wrote
of a certain character in his *Joan of Arc:* "He was king-bee of the little
village." The expression comes down from the time when the ancient Romans were still under the impression that the ruler of the beehive is masculine. Early English writers took it over from them, and there are quotations
applying the term "king" to the queen bee as late as 1710. We Missourians
must have been just a little slower than elsewhere to learn that are no
"king-bees," either in the beehive or in the American home.

Apparently the term "hog-eye" once signified in Missouri a small com-
pact place sunk in a hollow. Once we had two places named *Hog-Eye,* doubtless for this reason; but both of them have since disappeared from the map.
One of them, in Vernon County, grew too large to be any longer fittingly
described as a hog-eye—or at least it thought so. Hence, when it was incorporated in 1855, it adopted the more glamorous name of *Nevada* from the
golden West, though it has always insisted upon using a distinctive pronunciation of its name. The other, in St. Francois County, has found a cleverer
disguise. Although old documents prove that its original name was *Hog-Eye,*

and although its name is still so pronounced, it spells itself since 1890 as *Haggai,* after the Old Testament prophet. This is a signal example of progress from pork to piety.

A large proportion of the territory of Missouri, however, is still recognized as the property of the Devil, if place names are sufficient evidence of ownership. More than 30 localities attest the healthy respect we have for His Satanic Majesty. We have the *Devil's Elbow,* the name used for a sharp river bend; one of his *Boots,* in a boot-shaped cave in Warren County; three *Devil's Dens* and two *Devil's Tea Tables,* great smooth flat slabs of rock; a *Devil's Washpan, Washboard,* and *Wash Basin.* Five pieces of his *Backbone* are found in as many different counties. The *Devil's Toll Gate* stands in a narrow opening at the foot of *Taum Sauk Mountain;* and the *Devil's Race Ground,* a difficult rapid in the Missouri, was mentioned with awe as long ago as May 24, 1804, in the journals of the Lewis and Clark Expedition.

We even have three towns named for race horses: *Cliquot, Dexter,* and *Ortiz;* and at least one, *Flip,* for a pet dog. But the story that *Rolla* received its name from a dog is one that I refuse to accept.

The perennial struggle waged by our local postmasters with the Post Office Department in Washington has provided some of our best place-name jokes. One harried postmaster was instructed that he must find a name that was peculiar; another that he must select a name that would avert confusion; another that he could use any name protem until he had made up his mind; and still another that the number of names he had already sent in was enough. In humble obedience to their instructions, the names of these four towns have become *Peculiar, Avert, Protem,* and *Enough.*

We may conclude this entertaining branch of our serious subject with the stories of three place names that have given us a special amount of trouble. The old town of *Seventy-Six* in Perry County still puzzles us. One of its best known citizens, Mr. James A. Worsham, author and humorist, has assured me in a genial letter that his town was not so named because it has 76 hills to the mile, nor yet because the total distance from its northern to its southern suburbs is only 76 feet, nor even because there are 76 Democrats living there for every Republican. The explanation he favors is that a certain steamboat captain struck a snag and sank his vessel just outside the landing there, and since it happened to be the 76th landing for that voyage, the town was named for the catastrophe. With all due respect to this ingenious theory, I am inclined rather to connect the name with that of another town called *Seventy-Six* in Clinton County, Kentucky. We happen to know that that town was named for the date of the Declaration of Independence.

It is an article of faith in Lawrence County that the name of its principal stream, the *Turnback River,* was derived from a historic incident: namely, that when the first party of explorers to enter the county in 1830 reached its banks, they became discouraged and "turned back" to their Tennessee homes. To me, however, this old yarn sounds like an afterthought, one of those "ex post facto" explanations so often invented when the real origin of a name has been forgotten. It is far more likely, I believe, that the stream took its name from some early settler or resident on its banks, perhaps lower down where it runs through Dade or Cedar Counties. He may have borne a German-American surname like Turnbach, Turnbeck, or even Dornbach, later distorted by "popular etymology" into Turnback. I must confess that I have not yet identified this hypothetical name-father. But I decline to believe that anyone who got that far into Lawrence County would ever have "turned back."

The place-name investigator sometimes comes upon bits of unwritten history with values that are human as well as philological. Such was the experience of the present writer in trying to solve the riddle presented by the little Shannon County village oddly named *Ink.* We knew the name had been chosen in the year 1886 by the first postmaster, Mr. George Shedd; but we had not been able to learn, nor could we imagine, just why he had selected that particular name. In the summer of 1938, I decided to visit the place and see what I could discover on the spot. I spent a delightful afternoon, talking with nearly half of its 31 inhabitants, and I heard an interesting story.

Back in 1886, it seems, the Post Office Department in Washington, in a rare fit of economy, had decreed that short names were desirable for new post-offices. Apparently a great saving in public funds could be effected in manufacturing the official "ring" or stamp which the national Postal Department sends out to each new office, if the length of names could be kept down to three letters. This part of the story is a bit hard to believe—that such economy was ever practised by the government in Washington. But it is a fact that a surprisingly large number of three-letter Missouri post-offices were established at just about that time. There are places not far from *Ink* that rejoice in such economical names as *Map* and *Nip* and *Rat* and *Not*—and there are good stories that could be told about each one of them.

At any rate, Mr. Shedd believed he was following official instructions in seeking a name with but three letters. In loyal compliance, he called in the entire community, and asked for suggestions. Some one produced a school primer for teaching children to read—one beginning, as they used to do, with two-letter words like a-b, ab, and proceeding to three-letter words like c-a-t, cat. All the three-letter words in that primer were gravely canvassed and discussed by the assembled citizenry; but not one of them seemed to them entirely satisfactory. What would one not give for a picture from the brush of a sympathetic artist like Grant Woods or our own Thomas Hart Benton of such typical Missouri democracy in action!

Just when it seemed that the meeting would have to be adjourned without a decision, some one accidentally knocked over and spilled the official ink bottle on the post-office counter. By the same motion, he provided an acceptable solution for their vexing problem. "Why not call our place Ink?" he blurted out. And the name thus nominated was unanimously elected.

We got about as close to the original sources, I believe, in solving the origin of the place name *Ink* as we well could. The only thing still lacking would be to inspect the original ink bottle. The obliging citizens promised me that they would try to find it and send it to me. If they ever do, we shall certainly give it an honored place in our projected Museum of Missouri History.

Aromatic Creek (Clark)—for Stinking Creek or Fox River
Avert (Stoddard), 1891
Bachelor Creek (Franklin)
Blackfoot (Boone) —for Perche Township
Buzzard's Roost (Franklin), 1852
Cliquot (Polk), 1890
"Constantinople" (Mark Twain's name for Palmyra)
Devil's Backbone (Jackson, Montgomery, Oregon, Phelps, Ripley)
Devil's Boot Cave (Warren)
Devil's Den (Webster)
Devil's Elbow (Butler and Pulaski)
Devil's Icebox (Boone)
Devil's Race-Ground (Franklin), 1804
Devil's Tea Table (Cape Girardeau and Miller)
Devil's Toll Gate (Iron)
Devil's Wash Basins (Warren)
Devil's Washboard (Dunklin and Wayne)
Devil's Washpan (Barry)
Dexter (Stoddard) 1873
"Eden" (Dickens's name for Marion City)
Enough (Iron), 1918
Flip (Shannon)), 1915
Ginlet (Boone)
Gore (Warren)
Gunboat (Warren)
Hog-Eye (St. Francois)—for Haggai before 1890
Hog-Eye (Vernon)—for Nevada before 1855
Ink (Shannon), 1886
Jimtown (Clark)—for Eldorado
King Bee (Ripley), 1895
"Napoleon" (Mark Twain's name for Marion City)

"New Thermopylae" (Dickens's name for Hannibal)
Ortiz (Audrain)
Peculiar (Cass), 1868
Poker Hollow (Crawford)
Protem (Taney), 1870
Pucky-Huddle (Crawford)
Pulltight (Pemiscot)—for Maplewood
Reed's Defeat (Franklin), 1874
Seventy-Six (Perry), 1886
Shakerag (Warren), 1820
Slingtown (Warren)
Stringtown (found in 12 counties)
Tanglefoot (Jefferson)—for Festus
Terrapin Neck (Boone)
Turnback River (Lawrence, Dade, and Cedar), 1830?
Whoop-Up (Boone)—later known as Sapp
Who'd-a-Thought-It (Pemiscot), 1904

COINED NAMES (38)

This last group of Missouri place names might have been included with the humorous names just listed, except for the fact that they show more ingenuity than humor. They are all deliberate coinages out of fragments of words or letters stuck together somehow. They are part and parcel of the immense proliferation of names arbitrarily manufactured out of initials, like USA, USSR, UMT, GOP, ETO, and others, which are rapidly bringing our language back to the primitive agglutinative stage.

Old names that grow naturally are usually better than artificial coinages. But when the founders of a new place are suddenly called upon to provide it with a name, they sometimes make one up out of whole cloth, just as panic-stricken parents have been known to do for their hapless infants. The results of their misplaced ingenuity are often painful, sometimes excruciating, but occasionally rather clever.

Missouri has its full share of such manufactured names, or blends, as philologists call them. Places on or near state boundary lines have often been named by blending their abbreviations, as has been done with *Illmo*, *Moark*, and *Mokan*, formed in the same way as *Penmar* on the border between Pennsylvania and Maryland, or *Kenova* at the point where Kentucky, Ohio, and Virginia come together. Strangely enough, no one as yet seems to have tried to combine Iowa and Missouri, although *Iamo* would make a perfectly good name of the same sort.

County names have been welded together in the same way in *Mariosa*, *Gascozark*, and *Lorwood*, and the abbreviations "Co." and "Mo." have been used to form *Hico*, *Hocomo*, *Claycomo*, and *Taneycomo*. At *Arbyrd* the initials of a local landowner were combined with his name, and at

Ilasco the first letters of six ingredients used in the mixing of cement, which is the town's principal industry. Quite a number of towns have pieced together their names out of bits of the names of their founders, as in *Bucoda, Como, Lanton, Lecoma, Micola,* and *Walbert. Ardeola, Pascola,* and *Saco* are said to have been manufactured in some such way, but the priceless key to their cryptic significance has been lost. The founder of *Wardell* attached -dell to the first syllable of his name Warren, and the man who owned the land around *Winnetonka* joined what he supposed to be an Indian suffix -tonka to his own name Winn. Perhaps he modeled it upon *Hahatonka,* whose founder mistakenly thought he had derived it from Indian words meaning "smiling waters."

The inventor of a name has a prescriptive right to make it mean anything he wishes. The postmaster who coined *Dorena* said he formed it from a current slang term "doreen," meaning "money," which he thought might be lucky. *Ozora* was suggested by Ozarks. *Montevallo* is supposed to unite the Italian words for "mountain" and "valley." *Sereno* implies a quiet peaceful spot. *Knob Noster* is alleged to have been taken from the remarkable Indian mound or knob there, with the addition of the Latin "noster," meaning "our," suggested by a local school teacher. I suspect it was really a reworking by what is called "popular etymology" of the original Indian name of the mound, whatever that may have been. *Oronogo* arose, according to the local legend, from a drunken miner who stood up in town meeting and shouted, "Boys, by—, it's ore or no go." I have my doubts about the story, which is another of those popular yarns too good to be true, and think it more likely to have been a distorted Spanish name of that sort that were flooding into the State just at that time. *Wye City* is a jocular substitute for the letter Y, because two roads come together there in a Y-shaped angle.

Oddest of all in this group of oddities are the names that were formed backwards. Thus *Spurdod* reverses Dodd's Spur, *Rolyat* Taylor, and *Labinnah* Hannibal. The town of *Etlah* is said to have been so named by a company of weary German immigrants who believed they had found there at last a stopping-point or "Halte" in the long march they had made to escape from tyranny and oppression in their Fatherland. Perhaps they felt that by spelling the word backwards they might fittingly describe the topsy-turvy new world into which they had wandered.

Arbyrd (Dunklin), 1915—for Mr. A. R. Byrd, landowner
Ardeola (Stoddard), 1891—for several men now forgotten
Bloomfield (county seat of Stoddard), 1835—bloom plus field (because its founders saw a large field of flowers there)
Bucoda (Dunklin), 1915—for Buchanan, Coburn, and Davis, founders
Claycomo (Clay)—for Clay County, Missouri

Como (Henry), 1880—for Covey and Moberley, founders

Dorena (Mississippi), 1899—from "doreen," slang term for "money"

Etlah (Franklin), 1864—German "Halte" backwards

Fremont (Carter), about 1887—for A. J. Freeman, founder, plus -mont

Gascozark (Pulaski)—Gasconade River and Ozark Mountains

Hahatonka (Camden), 1897—for Indian "laughing waters" (?)

Hico (Dallas), 1904—for Hickory County

Hocomo (Howell), 1931—for Howell Co., Mo.

Ilasco (Marion), 1900—for Iron, Lead, Aluminum, Silicon, Calcium, and Oxygen, ingredients of cement made by the local Portland Cement Company

Illmo (Scott), 1905—Illinois plus Missouri

Knob Noster (Johnson), 1856—Knob plus Latin "noster" (?)

Labinnah Club (Marion), 1904—Hannibal backwards

Lanton (Howell), before 1860—for Lancaster and Sutton, founders

Lecoma (Dent)— for Lenox, Comstock, and Martin, founders

Lorwood (New Madrid), 1909—Lorain and Wood counties, Ohio

Mariosa (Osage), 1853—Maries and Osage rivers

Micola (Pemiscot), 1904—Michie and Coleman, founders

Moark (Dunklin), 1901—Missouri plus Arkansas

Mokan (Bates)—Missouri plus Kansas

Mokane (Callaway), 1849—for the M. K. & T. R. R.

Montevallo (Vernon), 1881—Italian "mountain" plus "valley"

Oronogo (Jasper) —(see above)

Ozora (Ste. Genevieve), 1901—from the Ozarks

Pascola (Pemiscot), 1894—coined by Louis Houck, how not known

Rolyat (Grundy), 1898—Taylor backwards

Saco (Madison), 1890—for two men, now forgotten

Sereno (Perry), 1889—meant to be a quiet place

Spurdod (New Madrid), 1918—Dodd's Spur backwards

Taneycomo Lake (Taney), 1914—for Taney Co., Mo.

Wardell (Pemiscot), 1903—for Warren, founder, plus "dell"

Walbert (Franklin), 1895—for Walter and Herbert, sons of the first postmaster

Winnetonka (Clay), 1935—for Winn, founder, plus -tonka to give an Indian flavor to the name

Wye City (Texas), 1933—a Y-shaped highway junction

UNSOLVED NAMES (64)

The solutions offered for a good many of the place names listed in the previous pages are more or less doubtful, as has been frankly admitted, with the reasons for uncertainty in each case. For the additional names listed here, most of which are in present use, and many of them for important places, we have no solution to offer at all. The obstacles have been either lack of information, because there was none to be had, or because the names were overlooked by the workers in our survey, or in some cases too much information, which is just as bad. When accounts of the founding or naming of a place are conflicting, or obviously mere speculative guesswork, it has seemed the part of scientific caution to withhold conjecture until at least some promising clue emerges. Perhaps some readers under whose eyes these pages may chance to fall will have suggestions for solving some of our remaining puzzles.

Abattis (Warren), 1886
Abo (Laclede), 1891
Abo (McDonald), 1886
Acasto (Clark), 1860
Aholt (Chariton)
Algoa (Cole)
Amoret (Bates), 1890
Amory (Clay)
Arab (Wayne), 1908
Argola (Lewis), 1883
Arnica (Cedar), 1882
Athelstan (Worth)
Axtel (Macon)
Azen (Scotland), 1879
Bona (Dade)
Cable (Reynolds)
Cadet (Washington), 1867
Canalou (New Madrid), 1902
Chilliticaux (Cape Girardeau)
Chula (Livingston), 1885
Cuivre River (Lincoln)
Deray (Cape Girardeau), 1900
Diecke (St. Louis)
DODGE COUNTY, 1846-1853 (absorbed by Putnam)
Donawali (Ripley), 1804
Faro (Madison)
Festus (Jefferson), 1886
Hardage (Shannon)
Kenoma (Barton), 1884
Keota (Macon), 1900
Kolano (Crawford), 1897
Lagonda (Chariton), 1881
Lahoma (St. Louis), 1909
Lakota (Cooper), 1901

Livonia (Putnam), 1859
Marmaton River (Bates and Vernon), 1839
Montague (Christian), 1900
Neongwah (or Niangua) River (Camden)
Nishnabotna River (Atchison)
Nixa (Christian)
Nodaway River (Nodaway)
Palmetto (Greene)
Pembina (Christian), 1885
Peruque Creek (Warren)
Pevely (Jefferson), 1860
Plad (Dallas), 1892
Ponca (Ste. Genevieve), 1910
Qulin (Butler), 1883
Raizon (Perry), 1899
Revere (Clark), 1889
Rolla (Phelps), 1858
Santuzza (Lewis)
Schluersburg (St. Charles)
Scopus (Bollinger),1897
Sequiota (Greene)
Simcoe (McDonald), 1894
Tarkio (Atchison)
Taum Sauk Mountain (Iron)
Tolona (Lewis), 1876
Tywappity (or Zewapeta) Bottoms (Scott), 1789
Wasola (Ozark), 1912
Weaubleau Creek (Hickory)
Wyeth (Andrew), 1895
Yama, or Yamma (Pemiscot)

Doubtless there are errors and omissions in the explanations that have been given; for scientific place-name study in America is still largely an untrodden path, and one beset by a host of difficulties. We have calculated that it is quite possible to make at least six mistakes in discussing any single place name: that is, in its spelling, its pronunciation, its location, its date, its name-father, and in the exact circumstances of its invention or adoption. Inasmuch as well over 1600 names have been at least mentioned in the course of the present study, that would yield a grand total of 10,000 possible errors that may have been perpetrated. We can only hope we have not gone wrong quite so many times, and plead with the poet Robert Burns that for the place-name worker

> to step aside is human.
> What's done we partly may compute,
> But know not what's resisted.

Any corrections, or additional information of any sort, that may kindly be supplied by anyone who is interested in this fascinating but perilous line of investigation will be most gratefully received, if communicated to the author,

CONCLUDING OBSERVATIONS

Our survey of the rich inheritance that has been stored up for Missourians in our place names, as they lie spread out before us in all their amazing variety of classes and categories, would not be complete without three final observations. These have sprung from a consideration of some of the larger problems which our names may help us to solve, and some of the uses we may make of all the verbal wealth in our storehouse. The first has to do with the changing attitudes toward some of our names that have developed during our two recent world wars. The second concerns the matter of tolerance toward the inevitable processes of Anglicization and Americanization which are always going in our orthography and pronunciation. The third touches upon the artistic question of the use that may be made of our place names by our poets and men of letters.

CHANGING ATTITUDES

The two world wars through which we have just passed have brought many changes in Missouri place names. There has been a natural and widespread aversion to any name that even sounded German or Japanese. But not all the alterations advocated will bear well the light of sober second thought.

The story has already been told of the agitation started after Dec. 7, 1941, to change the historic name of the little village of *Japan* in Franklin County (p. 35), and how the patriotic zeal of the agitators was checked when the true story of the name was revealed. It is to be sincerely hoped that all such names, which attest the cosmopolitan spirit of brotherhood that was felt by our ancestors toward all the nations and races of the world, and that has been so conspicuously illustrated on the map of our State, will remain where they are, in spite of national hatreds and bloody conflicts that temporarily alienate us from some of them.

Typical of what took place in 1918 is a story that comes from Bollinger County. A patriotic rally being held in the town of *Scopus,* to sell Liberty Bonds within the precincts of old *German Township*. "The quota for German Township," began the principal speaker, "is—by the way, I don't like that German name." "Neither do we," came cries from all over the house. Without more ado, it was voted unanimously to petition the County Court for a change of name to *Scopus Township*.

Probably very few of those present were aware that their township had borne its time-honored name for 118 years, or that it commemorated a historic event in the growth of the United States. When Colonel George Frederick Bollinger, on Jan. 1, 1800, at the invitation of the Spanish Government, led his 20 families of American colonists across the Mississippi and settled them along *Whitewater River,* he took a notable step toward the peaceful annexation of Missouri to the Union. All his people were of German or Swiss parentage, and the district they carved out of the new West was fitly named for them, as later on the county of Bollinger was for their able and devoted patriotic leader. It may be doubted whether much was really gained for the cause of liberty when their fine old name was replaced by the comparatively recent and meaningless name of *Scopus.* That name, by the way, is one for whose source and significance we have sought in vain.

Similar scenes were enacted all over Missouri, as they were in many other States, during the exciting war years. *German Township* in Madison County became *Marquand Township;* and the old *German Center School* in St. Clair changed its names to *Valley Center School. Keyser Avenue* in Columbia, on which I happened to reside, although it was named for an old family of English extraction, had its face lifted to *Wilson Avenue. Potsdam* in Gasconade County was rebaptized, more excusably, as *Pershing.*

Far fewer have been the changes made during the second war with Germany than in the first. Efforts to alter the name of *Kaiser* in Miller County to *Success* were unsuccessful; and so were those to replace *Diehlstadt* in Scott County by *Liberty,* which remind us of the equally futile attempt to rename that grand old German dish of "sauerkraut" by what would surely have been quite indigestible "liberty cabbage." It has gradually been realized that we were not fighting the glorious German heritage that has helped so much to build up our own commonwealth, nor the priceless spiritual wealth that has come down to us from Luther and Beethoven and Goethe, but merely the Nazi conspirators who tried to pervert that inheritance. We have all come to recognize that, Teutonic or not, there are no better American names now to be found anywhere than Stassen or Einstein or Eisenhower.

Language Tolerance

An eloquent appeal has come from beautiful *Bellevue Valley* in Iron County that a crusade be started to save its name from being "butchered" by journalists to Belleview. The French who settled here in 1795 spelled it Bellevue, writes this crusader, and that is too long ago to give up to the ugly spelling Belleview now. Can nothing be done to stop this criminal offense against history and orthography?

Much as I am opposed to crime in all its forms, and much as I relish, incidentally, that pleasant sense of superiority that any opportunity to exhibit one's knowledge of French brings with it, I am afraid that in this case I must take sides with the iconoclasts. So many good old French names have altered their spelling in the same way, as *Ozarks* for Aux Arks, *Smackover* for Chemin Couvert, *Sniabar* for Chenal Hubert, that we could not possibly turn back the clock now even if we would. And after all, why should we? We no longer even try to pronounce *Bellevue* exactly as the

French do; why should we continue to spell the name as if it were still French? When we take a name out of a foreign language into our own, surely what matters is not so much what it came from, as what it is coming to be. It may have been French once; but it is American now. The sooner it is completely naturalized the better.

When we try to halt the operation of the laws of nature, or of language, we are like old Mrs. Partington, whose veracious adventures were told by Sidney Smith. Once, it will be remembered, she had built her house a little too near the ocean; and then, when the tide began to rise and intrude into her parlor, she tried to sweep it out with her broom. It might be better to let the tide come in as fast as it likes, and even to welcome its arrival. Of course, we cannot hurry the tide. Deliberate efforts to reform or improve the language are usually ridiculous. They are much as if Mr. Partington had opposed his wife's efforts by swimming out to sea and trying to splash the tide in more rapidly. The old rule still holds: we need not be the first by whom the new is tried. But surely we ought not, like so many worthy English teachers, be the very last to lay the old aside.

What we can and ought to do is surely to throw our weight, whenever there is a real conflict of usage, on the side of our own language and its innate, natural tendencies. Why should so many self-appointed authorities champion always the backward-looking ideal of "purity" and exoticism in language, rather than the forward-looking ideal of Anglicity or Americanism? Is it not unfortunate, to say the least, that a good many teachers of English suffer the same affliction as Walter De la Mare's poor Jim Jay, who "got stuck fast in yesterday?" Perhaps that is the reason why teachers, as a class, have so little actual influence upon our living, changing language.

If ever we do learn to face forward instead of backward in out attitude to language, a host of our conventional judgments about place-name changes will certainly be reversed. When a wide-awake journalist ventures to Americanize *Bellevue* into *Belleview*, we shall praise him instead of prosecuting him. He is merely following in the track of those fearless early Missourians who gave us the sensible spelling *Ozarks* for Aux Arks, and of the French themselves, who vastly improved the Indian tribal name of the Wa-zha-zhe by turning it into *Osage*. We shall honor those later Americans who taught us to pronounce the *s* in *St. Louis,* even if the French did leave it out; and we shall understand why they still leave the *s* out in pronouncing *Louisville,* just because it is a younger town, which has not yet had quite enough time to become thoroughly Americanized. Whenever natural English pronunciations of French places like *Paris, Rheims,* or *Marseilles* have grown up, we shall firmly resist the pedants who would require us to struggle painfully, and never quite successfully, to reproduce the foreign speech sounds and accents. Much ridicule was poured on the head of the British Tommies in the First

World War who said *Wipers* for Ypres, but only by critics who did not know
that their ancestors had so pronounced the name for centuries before them.
Byron always pronounced the title of his greatest poem as "Don Joo-an"—
and his example ought to be good enough to justify the people of Franklin
County for calling *La Jolla Park* "Lah JAH luh" (laˈdʒalə) instead of something like "Lah Ho yah" (laˈhoja) as the Californians still struggle to do.
These heretical remarks, I am aware, will irritate the Mrs. Partingtons who
may read them. If so, let all their brooms descend upon my devoted head.

PLACE NAMES AND POETRY

Is there any beauty, or romance, or stuff for poetry, in our Missouri
place names? The author of the first volume of poetry ever published west
of the Mississippi River did not think so. Said Angus Umphraville, in a
special footnote to his poem "The Queen of Rivers," published at St. Louis
in 1821:

> The task of describing the course of the Missouri is rendered
> peculiarly disagreeable by the mean, low, absurd, inharmonious,
> and unappropriate names which white traders and discoverers have
> conferred upon its most romantic beauties. . . . What poet would
> not be deterred by such barbarous names from celebrating "The
> Beauty of the Cannonball," or "The Maid of Boone's Lick," or
> "The Hero of the Conewango?"

Later lovers of poetry modified this harsh judgment far enough to find some
romance and beauty in our foreign names, French, Spanish, and especially
Indian—such names as *Gasconade* and *Crève Coeur, Molino* and *Potosi,
Onondaga* and *Niangua;* and they began to plead wistfully for more of them
to replace the raw, crude, hopelessly American names that prosaic Anglo-
Saxon pioneers persisted in scattering over the landscape.

But time takes curious revenges. Nowadays poets have learned to find
beauty in unlikely places. Some of the foreign place names so much admired
a generation ago are still pleasant enough, but others among them retain
only a sort of pinchbeck beauty. As Stephen Vincent Benet has taught us:

> Seine and Piave are silver spoons;
> But the spoon-bowl metal is thin and worn.

Anybody can find poetry in springtime and sunsets. But it takes a real poet
like Robert Frost to find poetry in building a wall, and a real painter like
our own Thomas Hart Benton to make pictures out of barbecues and bap-
tizings, Huck Finn and Jesse James, and Frankie and Johnnie. After all,
sweat is a far more poetical word than perspiration.

So we may quote a few additional lines from Benet's classic, "American
Names," which has so fascinated our Missouri place-name workers that most
of them have placed it on the opening pages of their eighteen theses:

I have fallen in love with American names:
The sharp, gaunt names that never get fat;
The snakeskin-titles of mining-claims;
The plumed war-bonnet of Medicine Hat,
Tucson and Deadwood and Lost Mule Flat. . . .

I will remember Carquinez Straits,
Little French Lick and Lundy's Lane,
The Yankee ships and the Yankee dates,
And the bullet-towns of Calamity Jane.
I will remember Skunktown Plain. . . .

I shall not rest quiet in Montparnasse.
I shall not lie easy at Winchelsea.
You may bury my body in Sussex grass;
You may bury my tongue at Champmedy.
I shall not be there. I shall rise and pass.
Bury my heart at Wounded Knee.

Witness also the testimony of Mr. Dennis Murphy, one of the most genuine of recent Missouri poets, in his little volume of 1941 entitled *The Doomed Race:*

Willow Springs, Lebanon,
　　Mountain View, Cedar Ridge—
Crooked creek and highway run
　　Side by side to the bridge.

Asters by an old board walk;
　　Blacksmith's shop; grocery store
Where men-folks tipple, women talk,
　　And lazy hounds loll at the door. . . .

Evening Shade, Buffalo,
　　Rocky Comfort, and Birch Tree—
It matters little where I go;
　　Ozark towns keep haunting me.

Another of the younger Missouri poets, Mr. Ralph Alan McCanse, has demonstrated effectively in his two volumes, *The Road to Hollister: a Hill-Country Pastoral,* of 1931, and his latest volume published only last year, *Waters Over Linn Creek Town,* that many a place name is a compressed poem in itself. His earlier volume captures the spirit of Taney County as carried in its names:

　　　　　　　　A Sabbath air
Through all the hills prevailed. Across the Ridge
Came scarce a breath of wind, that morning hour;
And drowsy peace possessed the countryside . . .

But in the country stores—at Garber Bald,
Bee Creek, and Flag and Notch the people talked . . .
    of the big new dam
That turned White River into a lengthy lake,
Stretching for miles . . .
There's Dewey Bald; there's Hollister, and The Hill!

This is the silent epic of the hills:
The ancient Earth conceives; and Time fulfills.

In his *Waters Over Linn Creek Town,* he has interpreted even more appealingly the "spirit of place" and the very human people of

Camden and Hickory, and then Osage—
Then Morgan—Benton—each of them the stage
Where life ran quietly from day to day . . .

The ancient sleeping Ozark countryside . . .

Linn Creek that was; Zion; and Sycamore Mill;
All regions under the lake now, passing still . . .

Rivers and creeks throughout a host of hills
That now a winding man-made lake-bed fills:
The Osage, Turkey, Tebo, 'Tater, Lick
Moccasin, Mossy, Linn, and Forky Stick;
The Indians' cool Ne-Ong-Wah ('Many Springs'?)
The Buffalo, Gravois, Grand Glaize: perished things! . . .

The vision that saw Linn Creek town,
Linn Creek and Wayham and Purvis drown,
And Gladstone drown—those human places
Down in the fatal valley spaces . . .

And hundreds of hollows and leafy dens,
Honey Run, Crabtree, and Rainwater glens;
The blackberry patches and hazel stock
At Bee Hive, 'Possum, Standing Rock . . .

Count up to twenty streams, and more,
And the Vision will count you still a score . . .

Come: keep the low song till the end; take time
To linger in still places . . .

Apparently a hundred years of history and hard use have added a tang and a flavor to our most commonplace names that would have opened the eyes of old Angus Umphraville. Age enriches old paintings with what painters call patina. Perhaps our Missouri place names are gradually acquiring a sort patina too.

Mr. W. H. Auden, the distinguished British poet who has recently become an American citizen, has just coined a new word which will be a godsend in this connection. It is "topophile," for a lover of places. Somewhat intolerantly, however, Mr. Auden denies to Stephen Vincent Benet the title of a true topophile. When Benet rings the changes on Medicine Hat, or on "Tucson and Deadwood and Lost Mule Flat," and begs us to "bury his heart at Wounded Knee," the reader is not convinced, says Auden, that Benet had ever been at that picturesque place in South Dakota, or would have liked it if he had. It remains, Auden declares, just a pretty name on a historical map, like Milton's sonorous geographical name lists.

Mr. Auden would hardly allege that our young Missouri poets Murphy and McCanse have never been at any of the Ozark places they love to enumerate in their poetry. And to rule out John Milton from his exclusive list of genuine topophiles is surely a high-handed proceeding. Milton was the prince of all place-name poets, with his

> Thick as autumnal leaves that strow the brooks
> In Vallombrosa

and his

> All who since, baptized or infidel,
> Jousted in Aspramont, or Montalban,
> Damasco, or Marocco, or Trebisond,
> Or whom Biserta sent from Afric shore
> When Charlemain with all his peerage fell
> By Fontarabbia

not to forget his incursions into the North American continent, with

> the snow
> From cold Estotiland

and

> Now from the North
> Of Norumbega, and the Samoed shore.

Milton may have seen all these localities only in his inward eye; but assuredly he could make their names sing for us like organ notes, and could turn places into compressed poems as no other man has ever done.

Mr. Auden defines a true topophile as a poet who could write lovely poems about such New York spots as Stouffer's Teashop, Schrafft's Blue Plate Special, the Brighton Beach Line, or the General Theological Seminary. Just why he restricts his topophile to city names I do not quite understand. If so, St. Louis topophiles might pass muster by singing about such fascinating places as the *Eads Bridge,* the *Soldan High Schol, De Balivière Avenue, Garavelli's Restaurant,* and *Stix, Baer & Fuller.* We are well aware that modern poets like Auden choose words for their denotation rather than for their connotation. They dislike all words with overtones, and prefer the flat music of the tuning fork to the reverberations of the organ. The bees in their poetical hive are always lean and hungry, stripped for action as they issue forth to their daily task, never loaded with spoil and crusted with wax and honey as they stagger home weary at evening, as Milton and the Victorian poets liked them best.

For the "hollow men" of our exhausted age and our jaded city dwellers, they may be right. Our own T. S. Eliot has taught us what unexpected poetry there may be in such a line as

Not with a bang but a whimper,

or in describing a sunset as

Like a patient etherized upon a table

or even in the "damp souls of housemaids." We admire Auden's crisp modern vocabulary of "adrenal courage" and "the intolerable neural itch," or such packed and nervous lines as

Lecturing on navigation while the ship is going down.

Perhaps, however, he forgets that what he himself has called "the following wind of history" will soon put wax on the wings of his starchiest words. Milton's names, when they too were modern, doubtless seemed as bare and as tinglingly electric as Eliot's or Auden's. And some day, if enough poets discover its ineffable beauty, Stouffer's Teashop may become as crusted with overtones as Vallombrosa.

Meanwhile we should like to keep both Milton and Auden, and even Benet, upon our shelves. If we are not to be allowed to call ourselves topophiles when we care more for place names than we do for the places themselves, we shall have to thumb our Greek lexicons and coin another impressive compound. But please, Mr. Auden, can we not be at one and the same time both topophiles and toponomatophiles?

PLANS FOR FUTURE PLACE-NAME WORK[1]

American place-name study now stands at a crossroads in its progress. Having lagged so long behind other countries in the exploration of our place names and the discovery of what they have to teach us, we are at last beginning to take this comparatively new field of linguistic study seriously as a science. Much of our earlier and highly tentative approach to the vast and uncharted sea of American geographic nomenclature has been like that of Augustine's child standing on the seashore and examining a few interesting shells picked up along the beach. Too often in the past, the making of amateur collections out of random specimens of toponymy has been, like philately or coin-collection, merely a dignified sort of boondoggling.

We are now beginning to put out to sea. New and better organized expeditions are being launched in many directions. Some of them are products of local initiative or individual ingenuity, still defective in their planning, one-sided and unbalanced. If we Americans are the last to enter the new field of exploration, we must compensate for lost time by learning how to use and adapt to our needs all the best devices and methods invented and tested in other lands. Above all, we must make our work measure up to a new set of exacting and expert standards, improving on them if and where we can.

Any worth-while study of place-names must be a combination of geography, history, and linguistics. It is not a science at all without an adequate respect for geography and history. Geography in this connection means that the physical aspect of each place studied—its situation, area, landscape, and material resources—must be thoroughly known and sufficiently considered. Aid must often be sought from the kindred sciences of geology, botany, zoology, mineralogy, and agronomy. Nearly always the place must be actually visited by the investigator before the bearing of all the physical factors that so often lie unsuspected behind the origin and significance of its name can be adequately estimated.

Yet here there is almost as much danger of doing too much as too little. The student of place names must remember that he is not writing a gazetteer, nor should he attempt to do the work properly belonging thereunto. He must resist the temptation to which some of our great American dictionaries of common words have yielded, the combining of a fairly good dictionary with a second- or third-rate encyclopedia. Words and things have no legitimate right in the same volume, nor have place names and places. Not "Wörter und Sachen," but "Wörter" with only so much

---

1 Several paragraphs in this section are reprinted, with modifications, from the "Foreword" by the present writer in F. G. Cassidy's *Place Names of Dane County,* 1947.

"Sachen" as a full understanding of the words calls for should be our aim. It is always better to tackle one task at a time.

Respect for history means above all a respect for dates. We must discover if possible the exact date when the place name was adopted or invented, must test all its possible origins by a comparison of dates, and if the name is obsolete, must do all we can to find out just when it was changed or disused. If precise dates are unobtainable, we must at least set down the dates of its earliest and its latest recorded use, and arrange all the successive alterations in its form, spelling, pronunciation, and significance in their chronological order, as the English Place-Name Society has so well done with its material. Then with the correct chronology as a framework, we must record all that can be learned about the circumstances of its origin, the person or persons responsible, and the reasons or motives that led to its adoption, its alteration, and its passing out of use.

Our history must include the economic and sociological factors, which are often so much more important than the political for the place-name investigator. Above all, it must keep an eye open for folklore and legend, which often offer factitious and "ex post facto" explanations for the names, but sometimes furnish, under the guise of fiction, useful clues to the real facts, and which, whether fact or fiction, frequently shape and control their forms and fortunes. Naturally we are often able on matters of detail, circumstantial, historical, or personal, to do far more than our European colleagues could ever dream of doing; and we must take full advantage of our greater closeness to our beginnings. Yet here again we must remember that we are not writing history, but merely using history for our purpose. Many items of local or regional or national interest, however fascinating in themselves, must be sternly eliminated if they are irrelevant to our central problem of naming. We must hew to the line, without stopping to pick up the flying chips unless we really need them.

Geography and history are basic and indispensable in our work; but of the three fundamentals the greatest, after all, is linguistics. When we have extracted all the help available from the special sciences that deal with space and time, without yielding to the temptation of trying to become geographers or historians ourselves, we must never forget that we are primarily engaged upon a linguistic investigation. Nor must any of the branches of language study be neglected. The student of place names is concerned not only with etymology, but also with phonology, semantics, word-composition, and dialectology.

This means that the treatment of a place name will remain inadequate until it is thoroughly studied not only as a name but as a word. We must try to understand all its sound changes and sense changes, and follow its development all the way from its parental language or dialect through the various steps it may have taken in the devious process of Anglicization, Americanization, and modernization. We must consider its component parts, and how they have been put together. We must also relate our subject to the study of American dialects—a field in which not much more serious work has been done, as yet, than in American place names. Here probably place names will have as much to give as to take. European students have already discovered that the dialect terms and forms used so characteristically and abundantly in place names are peculiarly illuminating, just because the names are exactly located and almost always fairly well dated. At any rate, these two largely unexplored domains will surely prove to have intimate connections.

Doubtless we shall find much more to learn about American place names as we extend the national survey now just beginning. The solution of problems that are insoluble in Missouri alone will emerge when we encounter parallel problems in Michigan or Tennessee or Texas. But we can strive for thoroughness, accuracy, and insight even in the limited field of a single State. Whatever limitations or restrictions may be imposed, we must make the investigation of our own particular corner a genuine "study in depth."

A Master-Plan for our Missouri Dictionary

We have, as has already been stated, in our card-file a total of 32,324 Missouri place names for which information has been collected in 18 theses produced in our Graduate School from 1928 to 1945 and covering the entire State. Since their completion, a few thousand additional names have been brought to our attention, making a grand total of approximately 35,000.

Our big problem now is to cut down and consolidate this unwieldy mass of material, so as to make out of it a single, manageable, and usable volume.

The task of selection and elimination will be a considerable one, but by no means insuperable. A very tentative estimate is that the proposed volume will need to include less than half of the places so far treated, i.e., about 15,000 or 16,000; and further, that these may be reduced to about 5,000 or 6,000 actual entries, by the consolidation of repeated and transferred names. Furthermore, by judicious pruning and condensation the size of these individual entries can and should be materially reduced. If both of these substantial reductions are accomplished, a volume of something like 500 or 600 pages may cover the ground adequately.

This process of severe selection and compression will involve two important steps. First will come the matter of selection. Here a somewhat arbitrary line must be drawn in determining our standards of admission. Probably it will be best to draw the line between what may be called the larger and the smaller names. My plan is to exclude, for the most part, all the "little" names: schools, churches, and cemeteries, roads and railroads, mills and mines, ferries, farms, and estates, industries and places of business, camps and houses, parks and streets, springs and ponds, caves and groves, mounds and knobs, and the smaller hills and islands. All of these except street-names are included in our present card-file, though by no means exhaustively. Their exclusion in the proposed volume may be justified on several grounds: first, the necessity of avoiding excessive bulk; second, the fact that we have not been able to get all of them; and third, because they are after all essentially private or individual rather than public or communal.

Some of these names are of great interest in themselves; and one provision will have to be made. When, as often happens, a "larger" name is derived from a smaller one, as in the case of a town or river from a school, church, or spring, the explanation of the larger name must be pursued, if possible, into the original source of the little name from which it was taken, even though the "little" name will not be given a separate entry. For example, the town of *Gilead* in Lewis County, named for *Gilead Church,* will have to include in its entry the Biblical origin of the church name; and the city of *Webster Groves,* which took its name from *Webster College* there, must explain how the college was named for Daniel Webster. In special cases, perhaps other exceptions will have to be made. But it is altogether probable that the omission of all or nearly all of these "little" names will reduce the total number of places to be included by one half or more.

Included will be the names of all cities, towns, villages, and post-offices or railway stations; all counties, townships, districts, and other civil divisions, but not voting precincts; all natural features large enough to appear on ordinary State or county maps, such as rivers, streams, creeks, branches, lakes, bayous, mountains, valleys, hollows; all other names listed in old or recent guides and gazetteers, including all the former names, whether now extinct or replaced, so far as they are discoverable; and also fictitious names, sobriquets, nicknames, legendary names, and the like that are or have been used for any of the actual places included in the above categories.

In the second place, the number of entries will be cut down materially by making a careful distinction between the places themselves and their names or name-elements. Only the distinct name-elements will be given separate entries. Thus such widespread favorites as Benton, Jefferson, Osage, Bethel, Pleasant, Cedar, Panther, Hollow, etc., each of which has been used in Missouri, alone or in combination, for a score or more towns, townships, streams, or mountains, will be entered and explained only once—of course with a list of the places using each of them appended.

In other words, each entry in the dictionary will be concerned with a particular name or name-element, not with a particular place. In this way the very large number of names that are compounds or combinations will be analyzed into their elements, which of course are far less numerous. *Kansas City,* for example, will be discussed under Kansas, along with all other names using the Indian tribal appellation; and City will be treated separately in its place, as a prime favorite among detached suffixes, for over a hundred Missouri communities, usually the smaller the better. So *Maryville* will appear under Mary and again under the attached suffix -ville.

One distinction will have to be made here, however: i.e., between the specific parts of such names, e.g., Kansas and Mary, and the generic parts, e.g., City and -ville. For the former all the full names using them will be listed and explained in the same entry. But the latter, the common place-name elements, though they will all be entered in their alphabetic places in the dictionary, will not require such full treatment. Only when they have some special sense or usage as Americanisms or Missourianisms, as many of them do, like City, Hollow, Bluff, etc., will they need to be explained; and no complete list of the places using most of them will be necessary. Some of them, indeed, run into the hundreds; for these merely illustrative examples will suffice.

There are several hundreds of these common place-name elements. Some are usually attached, as in the cases of *Benton-ville, Pattons-burg;* a larger number are detached, as in *Jefferson City, Poplar Bluff, Missouri River.* Some are prefixed, as in *Cape Girardeau, New Madrid, Lake Benton;* but most of them are suffixed. They give, more than anything else, to Missouri place names their characteristic flavor and individuality.

In this matter of analyzing the existing place names into their separate elements, we must distinguish between elements actually used in the formation of our Missouri names, and those found in other types of compounds or combinations. Thus *St. Louis, Black Hawk, White Cloud, King Bee,* and *Jay Bird* will be treated as units, not broken into their component parts; for they are not *place-name* compounds. Nor will *Birming-ham, Kinder-hook, Cap au Gris,* be cut up and treated separately; for they are *previously formed* compounds, brought to Missouri ready-made, and having no part in the actual building up of new place names in Missouri.

One other preliminary observation is needed here. Mere identity of form or spelling is not enough to make a single name; there must also be identity of source. The same rule will be followed as in the ordinary dictionary in determining the identity of a word. Homonyms of different etymology are different words, as in the case of *ball,* round object, which is Teutonic, and *ball,* social entertainment, which is of Romance origin. Thus *Swan Pond,* named for the bird, will have to be a different entry from *Swan Lake,* named for John Swan; and so must *Lincoln County,* named for General Lincoln of Revolutionary fame, from the town of *Lincoln* in Benton County, which was named for President Lincoln. On the other hand, a mere difference of spelling in two names of the same origin will *not* call for treatment in different entries: thus the great Indian name Osage, used in various combinations for over 25 places (County, River, Creek, Township, Lake, town, etc.) will include in the same entry all the variant spellings found in the *Rivière Ouschage, Hoozaw River, Huzzah* (Huzza, Hussah) *Creek,* and *Whosau Trace;* though of course we shall have to enter each of these variants in its alphabetical place with a cross-reference.

The second step in the troublesome process of compression will have to do with the material to be put into each entry. So far, in our eighteen theses, we have followed a much too liberal and inclusive policy. On the ground that it is always easier to pare down than to build up, we have admitted many interesting details of history, biography, topography, economic information, or local legend which our students came across, and which if excluded might be hard to recover. Now, however, is the time to cut down. For our proposed single volume to cover the entire State, our policy must clearly be one of rigid exclusiveness. We must remember that the book is to be a dictionary, not an encyclopedia. Names, not the places in themselves, are our object. The purpose of the work is fundamentally philological, not historical, topographical, nor factual. Here we shall adopt the policy of the Oxford English Dictionary or the Dictionary of American English rather than that of Webster, the Standard, or the Century, and try to produce a place-name dictionary that cannot be confused with a gazetteer or a compilation of local history.

Hence all historical, biographical, economic, botanical, zoological, topographical, or sociological data, and all mere information of any other sort, must be relentlessly pruned away, no matter how interesting it is in itself, unless it bears directly on the name itself and the reasons for its origin, or for its form and development, its changes, or its obsolescence and possible disappearance as a name. On the other hand, anything pertinent to the central problem of naming, such as its pronunciation, its phonological development, its etymological history, or its dialect idiosyncrasy, will have a rightful place in the work. We shall therefore include in each entry the following items, so far as they have been discoverable.

CONTENTS OF A TYPICAL ENTRY

Entries will naturally fall into three parts or divisions, which may be called the identification, the derivation, and the comment.

The first, identification, will include:

1) The name-element (in distinctive type).

2) Its pronunciation, given in the International Phonetic Alphabet, as modified in Kenyon and Knott's *Pronouncing Dictionary of American English.* The pronunciation will always be included where it is known, as

heard from the lips of the natural leaders in each community, with all local variants and their provenance. It will be omitted only for repetitions, for extinct names, and in other cases where for any reason the local pronunciation has not been secured.

3) The full name of the place or places using the name or name-element, with the number of occurrences prefixed. These lists, as noted above, are to be complete for all the specific elements, but not always for the generic elements, i.e., the place-name prefixes and suffixes, whether attached or detached. If comparatively rare, or of special importance for any reason, the full list may need to be supplied; but ordinarily prefixes and suffixes will merely be illustrated by a sufficient number of examples.

4) The nature or character of the place (town, post-office, county seat, etc.) if not indicated by the generic element of the name.

5) The location of each place, usually to be indicated by the name of the county where it is found. This may be omitted for places too large to need it, or for rivers and streams that pass through more than one county.

6) Dates, if discovered: when, or by what time, each place received its name; also, if the name is no longer used, the date of its disuse.

The second part, the derivation, will of course constitute the main and fundamental part of the entry. It will naturally include

1) The source or origin of the name. By this is meant its immediate, not its ultimate, origin. If it is a borrowed name, it means the identification of the place from which it is borrowed, with the country or the State where that older place is or was located. If it is a historical name, it means the event commemorated, with its nature and date. If personal, it means the complete name of the person, usually with his position, rank, or occupation and his biographical dates, together with any *relevant* facts of his life. If topographical or environmental, it means the significance, botanical, zoological, mineral, agricultural, etc., of the name, with any relevant facts about the landscape or natural surroundings. If cultural, it means the essential facts that explain the adoption or use of the name: e.g., for a literary name, the character of the work, its author, date, etc.

But we are not responsible for ultimate sources. For example, if the name is borrowed from a town in England, it will be sufficient to identify the British town, but its etymology may be left to the English Place-Name Society. For personal names, the person is the source, and no etymology of his name is called for. For names derived from a foreign language, such as Indian, French, or Hebrew, it will not be necessary to give the derivation or even the meaning of the word or name in the original language, unless that derivation was known to the namers of the Missouri place and influenced their selection. Thus *Missouri* will be traced to the Indian tribe so called, without trying to explain its very doubtful Indian etymology;

and *Salem* will be sufficiently explained by a reference to the Bible passage or passages identifying it with Jerusalem or with the Church; but it will be superfluous to mention its meaning of "peace," unless that significance was clearly in the minds of the Missourians who chose it as the name of the Missouri place.

2) The circumstances, or explanation, of why the name was chosen. Such details will vary, of course, with the nature of the name. They may be historical, biographical, topographical, cultural. Whatever may have been the reason or reasons why the name was selected—and naturally they are often not procurable at all—they will usually depend upon the giver of the name, or "name-father." Hence we must mention him or her, if we can, with his position in the community and his dates. If he is still living, as we American students of place names fortunately often find him to be, we can get the best evidence of all from his own lips. But whatever we are able to discover, we must prune away anything, no matter how interesting it may be in itself, that is not strictly pertinent to the problem in hand. In case the name has been changed or discarded, we must similarly try to give, if possible, the dates and circumstances of its disuse.

In this, the central part or essential heart of the entry, we must be scrupulous to distinguish doubtful or merely conjectural derivations or explanations from those that are fairly certain. My plan is to place a ? before any explanation that is doubtful— i.e., one for which there is some but no very good authority. An explanation or derivation that is purely conjectural will have ?? put before it. Names that are quite unsolved—i.e., those for which no source or explanation at all could be found, such as those listed above on pages 118 and 119 will have an asterisk placed before the entry. We should try to avoid the pontifical air of infallibility too often assumed by lexicographers, whose findings must rest, as our experience amply demonstrates, on very human and fallible evidence in a multitude of cases.

The third division of the entry may be called, rather vaguely, the "comment." This will be largely linguistic. It will have to do mainly with cases of variation in spelling or pronunciation, matters of dialect usage, cases of folk-etymology, contamination, or "blends," the influence of the language of origin, and the degree of Americanization. Other significant comment upon the significance, background, or later fortunes of the name, or upon other matters, may occasionally be appropriate, but only when unmistakably relevant.

The entry will be followed by references, in parentheses, to the essential sources of our information. These will usually be arranged in chronological order, beginning with original documents, maps, etc., then published books, articles, and previous studies, finally living informants, whether their information came by correspondence or by interview. To save space, abbrevia-

136

tions will be used as far as they can be made convenient and clear. The ideal to be aimed at is to make the parade of sources inconspicuous but adequate and intelligible to the ordinary intelligent reader. A careful table of all abbreviations used will be given at the end of the volume, along with a complete bibliography, in the general fashion followed in the volumes of the English Place-Name Society.

In addition to the main dictionary, the volume will contain an introduction at the beginning and a bibliography and certain indexes at the end. The Introduction, of which a sort of first draft has been attempted in the present bulletin, will be sharply condensed and should not occupy more than fifty pages. It will attempt to sketch the toponymic background and the significant results of our investigation, and will summarize with illustrative examples the chief classes of names represented: Borrowed, Historical, Personal, Topographical, Cultural, with their subdivisions. For some of the more important subdivisions, an effort will be made to furnish complete lists. Next will come a discussion of important special features of the names, especially the philological aspects: composition, orthography, phonology, dialect, linguistic origins, etc. (possibly with complete lists for some languages); also the chief factors concerned with changes of names; and finally a brief discussion of the sociological aspects, folkways, and folklore so richly exemplified in our Missouri place names.

The bibliography will be organized in its natural divisions, chronological order being followed within the various subdivisions; except that personal informants will be arranged alphabetically.

Perhaps no index at all will be needed, certainly none of place names, all of which, with all their parts and elements, specific and generic alike, will be listed under a single alphabet in the main dictionary. I have thought of two indexes as possibly desirable: an index of all persons commemorated, and an index of dialect terms and Americanisms, especially those not included in previous dictionaries.

SPECIMEN ENTRIES

Following are 25 specimen entries, of various kinds. All of these are fairly brief, and will represent the average length of the vast majority. After them are given five longer entries, where special problems have arisen, or where a large number of places are combined in a single entry.

Amanda (ə'mændə), Crawford; p.o. est. by 1857, after which year it was moved to the new town of Cuba (q.v.). Named by the postmaster George M. Jamison, for his wife. (Goodwin, 2; Goodspeed, 529; Munro)

Cornwall ('kɔrn,wɔl), Madison; r.r. station est. 1889. ?Said to have been named for the shire in England, because of the Sprowle Tin Mountain (q.v.)

hoax which was perpetrated nearby. Sprowle came from the English Cornwall, which has always been famous for its tin mines, more authentic than the mythical ones of Madison Co. (Campbell; Douglas, I.379)

Cottbus ('kɑt,bʌs or 'kɑtbəs), Howell; p.o. est. bef. 1886 by Dr. Charles Ludwig from Germany, and named for Kottbus, an important manufacturing town near Berlin. Disc. since 1911. Spelling and pronunciation were Americanized from Ger. 'kɔtbus. (PG; MHR, Jan. 1917, 175; Chapin, Vaughn).

Darien ('dærɪən), Dent; p.o. since 1889. Named by J. W. Barry, a lover of Keats, from his sonnet "On First Looking into Chapman's Homer," which ends with the famous line, "Silent, upon a peak in Darien." (PG; *Hist. Dent*, 597)

*Donawali, Ripley; an Indian village that once existed at the present site of Current View. It was a fur-trading post of considerable importance as early as 1804. Neither the source nor the meaning of the name have been ascertained. (Land Mark Club; Mrs. Arnold)

Durgen's ('dɔ˞gn̩z) Creek, Lewis. Named by John Bozarth (q.v.), who settled here in 1819. Said to be named (??) for an old horse of his, which wandered off and was drowned in the stream. Old residents maintain, however, that a family of Durgens, or Durkees, lived here; and it was sometimes known as Durkees Creek. The term *durgen* or *durgan* is a dialect word well known in Missouri for an undersized or inferior animal or person, related to the word 'dwarf.' Vance Randolph records it from the Ozarks as applied to a horse. Probably the creek was really named for the family, and the anecdote of the horse arose by way of folk-etymology, which may have changed its spelling also. (*Hist. Lewis*, 18, 153; Coues-Pike, 11, note; Lloyd)

Enough ('i,nʌf—*sic*), Iron; p.o. 1918-38. As the story goes, the first postmaster, G. A. Hartzel, had sent in nearly 200 unacceptable names for it, before the authorities in Washington called it Enough. (PG; Mrs. Hartzel)

Gilead ('gɪlɪəd), Lewis; p.o. 1860-1904. Named for old Gilead Church, org. by the Missionary Baptists in 1833. A favorite church name, from Mt. Gilead, also called Mizpeh, where Jacob made his covenant with Laban (Gen. 31). It is interpreted as meaning "Hill of Witness." (PG; Campbell, 309; Lloyd, Minter)

Green Gables ('grin ,geblz), Camden; a summer resort near the p.o. Edith (q.v.) since about 1915. Its glamorous name was probably inspired by Lucy Maud Montgomery's best-seller *Anne of Green Gables*, first pub. in 1908. The summer houses there are said all to have their gables painted green. (Huddleston)

Ivanhoe ('aɪvən,ho), Shelby; p.o. 1876-86. So named by the postmaster J. G. Burkhart, who had just finished reading Scott's novel when the petition for the p.o. was sent in. (PG; Burkhart, Winetraub)

King Bee (ˈkɪŋˌbi), Ripley; an abandoned mill, village, and p.o. (est. 1895). So named by Thomas L. Wright, mill-owner, to signify the importance of his mill, which was the largest in the co. at that time. The term is an Americanism in the sense of "supreme ruler, master, aristocrat"; cf. Mark Twain's *Joan of Arc* (II. vii. 236): "He was king-bee of the little village." Although not to be found in any dictionary of Americanisms, it is recorded in *Dialect Notes*, vol. IV, from Virginia; see also the *Mark Twain Lexicon*, Ramsay and Emberson, 1938. It is a figurative application of the obs. *king-bee* for "queen bee," cited in the OED as early as 1679. Earlier English writers, after the Latin, labored under the misapprehension that the ruler of the hive was masculine; citations applying the term *king* to the queen bee are given from about 1386 to 1710. The name of the village is also written King-bee (PG; Langford, Slayton)

Louisiana (ləˌwizɪ'ænə or luˌizɪ'ænə), Pike; oldest town in the co., settled in 1816; co. seat till 1823. Named for a girl, Louisiana Basye, afterwards Mrs. David L. Tombs, born in St. Louis in 1804, the year when Louisiana Territory became a possession of the U. S. She is said to have been so named because she was the first child born in St. Louis after the Purchase. Her father, John Walter Basye, brought his family to Pike Co. in 1818, the year when the new town was definitely laid out, and the settlers honored his 14-year old daughter by naming it for her. Beck says it was at first called Louisianaville, but it was never known by that name. (Beck, 243; Bryson)

Mexico (ˈmɛksɪˌko), Audrain; co. seat: laid out Apr. 1836. Named for the country, in recognition of the increasing excitement over the independence of Texas from Mexico, which had just been achieved by the victory of Gen. Sam Houston at San Jacinto. (Campbell; *Hist. N.E. Mo.*, I. 186, 223; Vivion)

Oregon (ˈɔrɪgən or ˈɑrɪgən) County; org. Feb. 14, 1845, from Ripley Co. Named for Oregon Territory, in the midst of the exciting controversy with Great Britain over its possession, which was settled in favor of the U. S. in 1846. (Campbell, 407; Goodspeed, 181; MHR, Apr. 1917, 337)

Palmyra (pæl'maɪrə), Marion. Laid out in 1819; co. seat since 1827. Named by its incorporators for the ancient city of Mesopotamia, known as Tadmor in the Scriptures, founded by King Solomon (II. Chron. 8:4). They chose it because, like the city of old, their new town was to be the fertile heart of the "Two Rivers' Country" (q.v.). Mark Twain poked gentle fun at its grandiose name when in his *Tom Sawyer* he renamed it "Constantinople" (q.v.). Other sobriquets it has enjoyed have been "City of Flowers" and "Athens of Missouri" (q.v.). (Wetmore; Hayward; Goodwin; Campbell; *Hist. Marion*, 80)

Passover ('pæs,ovɚ), Camden; p.o. 1904-30. It is unlikely that a town would have been named directly for the Jewish feast. ??Probably the name was due to popular etymology from some early citizen named Passauer, Passche, Paschke, or the like, although no positive evidence to this effect has been secured. But cf. the similar distortions in the names of nearby places Rain Water Hollow, from Wrainwater, Right Point from Wright, Zebra from (?) Zieberer, etc. (PG; Williams, 345; Schrimsher)

Plevna ('plɛvnə), Knox. First laid out in 1877, and so named for the Bulgarian town where in that year the Russians defeated the Turks, after a siege of 143 days. The name seems to have been chosen by John Naylor, nicknamed "Plevna" Naylor, who is said to have started the town. (Campbell; Eaton; Stout)

Pulaski (pə'læskɪ or pə'læs,kaɪ) County, org. 1833. Cf. also the community called Pulaskifield in Barry, est. ab. 1902, formerly Bricefield (q.v.), and the p.o. of Pulaski in Ripley, 1913-35, now renamed Mullen (q.v.). All three were named for Count Casimir Pulaski (1748-79), Polish nobleman who fought with the Americans in the Revolutionary War and fell at the Battle of Savannah. Both the Barry and the Ripley communities were largely Polish settlements. At least 20 other places in 15 different States bear the Count's name. (Laws of Mo., 1833; *Ozark Region and People*, 70; *Hist. Laclede*, 113; Reed, Lane. For Pulaskifield, Mrs. Hadley, Mrs. Jones; for the Ripley p.o., PG; Butler, Langford, Young)

Quercus ('kwɝkəs), Butler; an important switching point for lumber on the Butler Co. R.R. Name given by W. N. Barron and Charles Langlotz in 1906, from the Latin botanical name for "oak." Oak trees were the principal source of timber in the co. (Campbell, 108; Barron's letter in *Intro. to Survey of Mo. P.Ns.*, 36; Pottenger)

Quincy ('kwɪnsɪ), Hickory; p.o. since 1867. It was platted and probably named in 1848. ?Probably for President John Quincy Adams (1767-1848), who died in Feb. 23 of the year it was laid out. There are 18 other places bearing the sixth president's middle name, which was favored by his admirers to distinguish him for his father President John Adams. (PG; *Hist. Hickory*, 68; Eaton)

Minnith ('mɪnɪθ), Ste. Genevieve; p.o. since 1886. It lies in the center of a rich wheat-growing district. Named by Judge Miles A. Gilbert of St. Marys for the Biblical city in the land of Ammon, e. of the Jordan, of which Ezekiel (27:17) wrote: "They traded in thy market wheat of Minnith"; cf. also Judges 11:33. (PG; Coffman)

Texas ('tɛksəs) County; also T. Twp. in Dent Co. The co. was org. in 1843 under the name of Ashley (q.v.), but was changed by act of the State Leg.

on Feb. 14, 1845, to Texas, in honor of the annexation of the Republic of Texas to the U. S. in that year. Many men from this section of Missouri had already emigrated to the new State, and many had enlisted for Doniphan's famous march of the Missouri men into Mexico which took place the next year. Perhaps the fact that, just as Texas is the largest State in the Union, so Texas Co. is the largest county in Missouri, had something to do with the choice of the name. (Campbell; *Hist. Texas,* 430; MHR Jan. 1933, 170)

Tiger ('taɪgɚ) Fork of North River, Shelby. ??Said to have been so named in 1835, when two panthers were killed on its banks, so large the settlers thought they were tigers. But places are rarely named for mere incidents. (*Hist. Shelby,* 633; Eaton)

Tranquillity (træn'kwɪlətɪ), Clark; p.o. in 1902. Doubtless an ideal name. The village was so tranquil that the p.o. was discontinued the following year. (PG; Buck)

Troublesome ('trʌbl̩səm) Creek, Knox and Marion. So named by 1874, because when other streams in the vicinity were tranquil, it was apt to be raging after a shower, and often rose out of its banks. (Campbell; *Hist. Marion,* 748)

Here are some longer entries:

Benton ('bɛntn̩). 37 places have this name in Missouri:
>   Benton, co. seat of Scott, 1822
>   Benton County, org. Jan. 3, 1835
>   Benton, proposed as name for co. seat of Buchanan in 1840, but
>   rejected on political grounds in favor of Sparta
>   B. Station on Mo. Pac. R.R. in suburban St. Louis, 1852, and B.
>   Park in s. St. Louis some time later
>   B. Barracks, St. Louis, during the Civil War, 1860-64
>   B. City, Johnson, 1872 (now disappeared)
>   B. City, Audrain, 1881
>   Bentonville, Benton, p.o. est. 1891 (perhaps named for the co.)
>   Lake Benton, name assigned by act of the State Leg. in 1931, but
>   superseded in popular usage by the name Lake of the Ozarks
>   17 B. Twps: Greene, 1833; Polk, 1835; Lewis, 1836; Linn, 1838;
>   Daviess, 1840; Wayne, by 1840, renamed North Benton in
>   1890; Adair, 1841; Andrew, 1841; Dallas, 1841; Osage, 1841;
>   Knox, 1845; Cedar, 1845; Texas, 1845, renamed Cass in 1850;
>   Stoddard, 1850; Webster, 1855; Atchison, 1858; Crawford, by
>   1870
>   11 B. Schools, in as many different cos.

An indefinite number of B. Parks, B. Streets, etc., could be added to the list. Cf. also Bullion's Landing and Bullion. All of these were named for Senator Thomas Hart Benton (1782-1858), who served in the U. S. Senate for 30 years (1821-51). Of the names, 16 were conferred during his term in office, when he was the idol of the State and widely known throughout the nation as the "Father of the West." The rejection of his name for the co. seat of Buchanan in 1840 showed that he had his enemies; and the change of name of the Texas Co. Twp. to Cass (q.v.) in 1850 marked the political struggle that overthrew him, when his opponent Lewis Cass won the Democratic nomination for President. But such later adoptions as Benton Barracks, the two Benton Cities, Bentonville, Lake Benton, etc., proved that he had by no means been forgotten. Judged by place names alone, he was the most famous of all Missourians. (PG; Campbell; Eaton; Garnett; Goodspeed; Douglass I. 108, 179, 290; Violette, *Hist. Mo.* 261-7; *Hist. N.E. Mo.;* Hists. of cos. mentioned; *Encyc. St. Louis,* 1879, I. 134-5)

Benton, Butler; R.R. station est. by 1874. ?For George H. Benton, attorney for the R.R. Now disused. (Campbell, 1066)

Benton, Dent; R.R. station, named for the Mark Bentons who entered land in the co. in 1836. (*Hist. Dent,* 568; Davis, 362; Keys)

Benton Branch, Dallas. ??For a local family. (State Highway Map; Bennett)

Benton Creek, Crawford. For a local family. (Campbell; Barton, Evans)

Bullion's ('buljənz) Landing, Marion: on the Mississippi at the mouth of the Fabius, by 1844. The name is often written without the apostrophe. Also the village of Bullion, Adair, about 1872, named partly for Benton and partly for C. H. Bull, a banker of Quincy, Ill., and a R.R. promoter. Senator Benton was known familiarily as "Old Bullion" because he stood for "hard" money, or specie currency. In the election of 1840, he led the faction of Democrats known as the "Hards" to victory over the "Softs," who stood for a liberal issue of paper by the "wildcat" banks. As a result of his success, Missouri was sometimes called the "Bullion State." (Rader, 78; Williams, 3, 20; Shoemaker, 147-55; Violette, *Hist. Mo.,* 261-67; Trimble)

-burg (bɜ·g). 88 places use this productive suffix. Some have been borrowed as wholes from Europe or from the East, as Altenburg, Hamburg, Strasburg, Chambersburg, Harrisburg; more have been freshly coined in Missouri, as Millersburg, Jeffriesburg, Martinsburg, Warrensburg, Gasburg. In 24 other places the same suffix appears under variant spellings: -berg 9 (Arnsberg, Bushberg, Frankberg, Frankenberg, Ehlenberg, Johannisberg, Jedberg, St. Johannisberg, Schoeneberg), -burgh 8 (Brownsburgh, Fredericksburgh, Lewisburgh, Mayesburgh, Petersburgh, Leasburgh, Wellsburgh, Schulersburgh—the last three with variant spellings in -burg); -boro 4 (Boonsboro, Clarksboro, Graysboro, Hillsboro); -borough 2 (Bensborough, Boonesborough); -bourg 1 (Louisbourg); -borg 1 (Swedeborg). All of these are pronounced like -burg, except -boro and -borough ('bɜ·ro or 'bʌro). The form -berg is found only in distinctively German settlements, where it began to make one or two new -berg names, but never thrived. Similarly -bourg is found only in one borrowed name of French origin, and -borg in one of Swedish. The endings -burgh, -boro, and -borough are distinctively of British provenance. Places in -burgh are in general older, and some of them have been altered to -burg. Mencken says that the U. S. Geographic Board has tried to shorten all -burghs to burg; but if so it has had far from complete success. The triumph of -burg in both spelling and pronunciation is probably not due, as has sometimes been asserted, to German influence, but came about merely as a "spelling-pronunciation" of the English -burgh, which is seldom so pronounced in the mother country. In Missouri it has become one of the most active and living affixes, applied to communities of any size; many of them are very small, some extinct, some merely projected. (DAE; Mencken, *Am. Lang.,* 473)

City ('sɪtɪ). Over 150 places use this favored affix: e.g., Benton C., Cement C., Des Moines C., Garden C., Kansas C., Mineral C., Monroe C., Prairie C., Washington C., Wright C. They vary in size from Kansas City with nearly half a million to many with a mere handful of houses, others extinct, some never more than projected. In one group of six western counties, 20 "cities" are to be found, of which 19 have fewer than 100 inhabitants. The name, in fact, as Johnson said of second marriages, is based in Missouri more on hope than on experience. Cf. DAE 2: "A grandiose or anticipatory designation for a mere hamlet or village." To the illustrative quotations there given may be added the following from Tixier's *Travels on the Osage Prairies* in 1840: "On the banks of the rivers in the United States an infinite number of towns can be seen which might well make one imagine an enormous population, if one did not understand the real meaning of certain words. It is fitting to remind the reader that one never sees hamlets, villages, or even towns in America. Any aggregation of houses is a city, and would rather do without a name than take another designation. This general claim makes the meaning of the word *city* much less precise than anywhere else." (p. 93). Not always, however, in a spirit of expansive optimism was the term appended to a name; sometimes it was added merely to distinguish : e.g., Benton City was probably so called merely because there was already a town of Benton; so Kansas City to distinguish it from the State of Kansas; cf. also Des Moines City and Washington City. The term is occasionally prefixed, usually in sobriquets, as "City of Flowers" for Palmyra, "City of Mineral Springs" for La Grange. But there was a tendency to reverse the order as time went on: thus the City of St. Charles became St. Charles City, now always simply St. Charles; and the town christened City of Kansas in 1853 was officially altered in 1889 to Kansas City. (DAE; Victor Tixier's *Travels,* trans. from the French and edited by J. F. McDermott, 1940)

Jefferson ('dʒɛfɚsṇ). 37 places have this name in Missouri (exactly the same number as are named for Senator Benton):

Jefferson County, org. Dec. 8, 1818
Jefferson City, Cole, capital of the State, 1822
J. Barracks, St. Louis, 1826
19 J. Twps: Cole, ?1822; Monroe, 1831; Clark, 1833; Johnson, 1835; Polk, 1835; Clinton, 1838; Buchanan, 1839; Daviess, 1840; Wayne, 1840; Grundy, 1841; Osage, 1841; Scotland, 1844; Cedar, 1845; Linn, 1845; Harrison, 1845; Andrew, 1846; Maries, 1855; Shelby, 1868; Nodaway, 1871
13 J. Schools, in as many different cos.
Also J. Station in Jefferson Co., prob. named for the co.
?Mount Jefferson, Carter

An indefinite number of J. Parks, J. Streets, etc., could of course be added to the list. All are named for Thomas Jefferson (1743-1826), President 1801-09. The county and the capital were so named during his life, as a personal tribute to the author of the Louisiana Purchase, which added the Territory of Missouri to the Union. Jefferson Barracks honored him in the year of his death. The others attest our continued veneration for the man who to Missourians will always be the greatest of all our Presidents. (PG; Goodwin; Campbell; Eaton; Parker; Wetmore; Hayward; Violette; the various co. hists. and atlases)

INDEX

Nearly two thousand place names treated in the preceding pages are here indexed, including about a hundred from outside the State which have been cited for illustrative purposes or for their Missouri connections. For these the location is added in parentheses; but for Missouri places the county is here added only in cases where two or more places in the State have used the same or nearly identical names. Sobriquets or nicknames are put in quotation marks. County names are capitalized.

An asterisk is prefixed to places that have disappeared or names no longer in current use. It is not always easy, however, to determine whether or when a name has vanished; the mere discontinuance of a post office, or the diminution in size or population of a place does not always mean the entire disuse of its name by its neighbors. Hence asterisks have been used sparingly.

148

152